REFLECTI
WITH
THE TESTIMONY OF DAN MCVICAR

Other books by the same author:

REFLECTIONS
FROM MOSES

WITH

THE TESTIMONY OF
DAN McVICAR

Hugh B. Black

NEW DAWN BOOKS
GREENOCK, SCOTLAND

© Hugh B. Black 1991

First published 1991 by
NEW DAWN BOOKS
27 Denholm Street, Greenock PA16 8RH, Scotland

All rights reserved.
No part of this publication may be reproduced,
stored in a retrieval system, or transmitted,
in any form or by any means, electronic, mechanical,
photocopying, recording or otherwise without the
prior permission in writing from the publishers.

ISBN 1 870944 10 0

Unless otherwise stated, biblical references are
to the Revised Version.

Cover design based on a painting by Marion Yorston Potter
Photographer: Craig Richardson

Production and Printing in England for
NEW DAWN BOOKS
27 Denholm Street, Greenock PA16 8RH, Scotland by
Nuprint Ltd, Station Road, Harpenden, Herts AL5 4SE.

This book is dedicated to those of my readers who eschew the easy ways of lower levels and aspire to the highest heights of spiritual endeavour.

Acknowledgements

I am grateful to my daughter Alison for editorial assistance; to my wife Isobel and to Miss Pauline Anderson, Mr Alistair Duff, Miss Jennifer Jack and Mr George Marshall for proof-reading and helpful contributions; and to Miss Ina Thomson, Alison, and Miss Irene Morrison for their respective parts in the processing of the material, much of it from tape-recordings.

My thanks are also due to the various authors and publishers whose works have been quoted.

Contents

Foreword

For more than twenty years I have been privileged to sit
under the ministry of the author and I have been delighted
to see this ministry reaching a much wider audience
through the publication of his books over the past three
years.

This latest book shows us not only the life of Moses but
the ways in which God deals with men (and women!) of
every age. The principles do not change although the
circumstances may differ. The aim is not simply to have us
meditate on Moses and learn about him, but to bring us
face to face with spiritual truths. The author is fond of
saying that preaching is not supposed to be an end in itself;
it is supposed to bring action—and this is as true of his
books as it is of his sermons. As you read through the
pages that follow you may find yourself growing uncom-
fortably aware that the objections which Moses made to
God are disturbingly like your own and the criticisms of
Aaron, Miriam and the others sound horribly familiar to
you! The book is not based on the past; it is based in the
eternal present and the I AM who spoke to Moses still
speaks to men and women today. Let Him speak to you as
you read and let Him show you the way into a deeper
relationship with Himself and a place where you can be
effective in His Kingdom.

The second part contains the testimony of Dan

McVicar. I first heard him speak many years ago when I was a child and his story was one of the most remarkable that I had heard at that time. Since then he has travelled much in Britain and abroad, working for God. I know that many people will be pleased to have this record of his story in print.

Jennifer A. Jack

Preface

This book falls into two parts:
1. The deliverance of Israel from Egypt with general reflections on the life of Moses.
2. The testimony of Dan McVicar, a well-known Scottish preacher.

The life of Moses is fascinating, and many spiritual principles may be derived from its study. As in *Reflections from Abraham*, an earlier book in this same series, the writing in Part 1 has been based on recordings made of studies presented at a Struthers Memorial Church camp at Wiston, Lanarkshire, a few years ago. No attempt has been made to deal exhaustively with the life of the great lawgiver: that is not the purpose of the book, which is rather to take particular events and learn from them something of the ways of God with men. There is, of course, a strong focus on the deliverance of Israel from Egypt.

Part 2 contains the testimony of Danny McVicar, a much-loved and much-travelled Scottish preacher. In recent books I have been including testimonies, and this has met with approval from many readers. Sometimes principles outlined in the first part of a book may be seen outworked in the lives of individuals. In Danny's case there is a very obvious connection. As Israel was in cruel bondage in Egypt, so was Danny McVicar in his own day in Scotland. Behind Israel's bondage stood Pharaoh and

11

behind Pharaoh Satan himself. Danny's life was firmly bound by that same evil power, but the day came when he was thoroughly converted, and from being a militant communist with a drink problem he became a much-used servant of God, free from the power of alcohol. As his testimony indicates, he preaches very widely across the country. God's work in his life has thrilled many thousands of people. He has been used in salvation, baptism in the Spirit, healing and deliverance. He is a twentieth century–first century man of God.

Danny was and is a rough diamond—indeed quite unique. His testimony is like himself. It's racy, it's punchy, it's pawky, it's colloquial; it breaks convention and it's none the worse for that. It doesn't give its story without diversion, but the diversions are often fascinating. It stands in the main as it came—with some of the more extreme Scotticisms modified for English ears, but not wholly eradicated.

PART 1

REFLECTIONS FROM MOSES

Introduction

The first part of this book outlines spiritual principles evident in the dealings of God with Moses. Many of these are of age-long significance: the calling and training of a man of God, the need for death to self and total submission to God, deliverance from the bondage of Satan in all its forms, and the consequences of rebellion. Aspects of truth such as the holiness of God sensed at Sinai and the power of intercession are significant in all generations.

We may learn much from a study of these and should apply the principles to our own lives today.

There is one word in the book title, however, to which I would draw particular attention—the word *Reflections*. We can become a reflective people, and there is a grave danger of stopping at reflections and never passing to a state of more positive action. Note that one of our basic reflections from the life of Moses relates to the demand which God made in that day and which He still makes. To Pharaoh He said: *Let My people go*. To every binding power He still says, *Let My people go*. Shall we turn again to Egypt and reconsider Israel's hour of deliverance, that we in our day may seek our personal deliverance? The basic message that Moses took to Pharaoh was simple and blunt: *Let My people go. Let My people go*. Pharaoh, instigated by the prince of darkness, said, *No, I will not let your people go!* And God said again and again and again, *Let My people go!* And Satan said, *I will not let Your people go.*

Note the determination, the persistence, the strength of the opposition of Satan, and the persistence and the strength of God. Stand back from the scene and view the repeated hardening of the heart. See the drama in its actual outworking. I am amazed at the persistence of Pharaoh. See that last fearful scene. The waters of the Red Sea are banked up. What a phenomenon: waters that should be flowing down are not—they are banked up. And Israel, at the command of God, is going through them. Pharaoh, seeing this, risks pursuit. In the fury of his determination he is regretting even at that last hour, even after the death of all the firstborn in Egypt, that he ever allowed the people to go. He is very tough; he has hardened his heart again. 'I will not give in, I will not give way, I will bring this people back into bondage!' I doubt if even as the rolling waters came in and he drowned in the depth of the sea he was fully broken. He may have died totally unrepentant. This reminds me of a very perceptive part in the writings of C.S. Lewis. In *That Hideous Strength* he depicts a man who had given himself deeply to evil, coming very near his end. There came a moment where there seemed to be the possibility of his making a right choice; there was a sudden flash of knowledge of the delusion under which he had lived, but in that critical moment it was too much for him to change course; he would not give up the illusion. Rather he plunged back into his delusion, and you almost feel him go screaming into hell...lost. Oh, the strength of the awful battle that lies beneath the surface, the battle between good and evil.

I want you to look again a little more deeply beneath the superficial appearance of things. Satan wanted to hold those people in bondage, to decimate their numbers, ultimately to obliterate them. And God said, *Let My people go*: He wanted to deliver them. Normally, when we read this, we may think, 'Oh yes, God wanted to take them out of bondage and into the land of promise.' That is as far as our thinking often goes; but that is only the very surface of things. As we enter the deeper spiritual world, we become aware that with God what was important was not just where Israel was dwelling geographically, whether Egypt or Palestine—but where they were and would be spiritually.

For us it is not a matter of where we dwell outwardly. God is not only wanting us to be free from obvious servitude, but He is wanting us to be free in the inner being. You remember the prophecy regarding Christ: *The Spirit of the Lord is upon Me ... He hath sent me to proclaim release to the captives ... To set at liberty them that are bruised* (Lk 4:18). God desires the liberation of the spirit, the liberation of the inner man, the full liberation of the sons of God. Those who have ever once known the joy of a free spirit will know the hell of bondage if they ever come into it again. Anyone who has ever known the wondrous freedom that comes from God is never again happy in all this world if he or she comes back into bondage. It is not possible. God's mind and will was to set His people free, and to bring them not only into a land of promise but into a liberty of spirit and a deep and living relationship with Himself.

1

Early Years

Before that hour when Moses stood on holy ground at the burning bush, God had chosen him to lead the children of Israel out of Egypt. By then he had been for forty years a refugee from that land. The hour of his commissioning had come, and for an understanding of that dramatic hour in history a knowledge of earlier background is helpful. In reviewing this we see the birth of a man of God, the training of a man of God, and something of the ways of God with the soul.

Abraham had been called of God from Ur of the Chaldees and came into Palestine the land of promise, the land that God had chosen for him and for his children. After a time famine came and Abraham went down to Egypt. While the Bible does not criticise him, neither does it indicate that he was in the will of God in doing this. He found himself in trouble in Egypt, and ultimately he came back to exactly the same place he had left, near Ai, the place of the altar. It looks as though he had gone round in a circle. In a later day God allowed his descendants to go down to Egypt and there they were cruelly enslaved for about four hundred years: I suspect that this was not unrelated to Abraham's earlier action.

The time came when God was minded to bring His

people out of Egypt. By then the Israelites had greatly multiplied in the land, and a day had come when a new Pharaoh arose who 'knew not Joseph', the man who had earlier saved Egypt and the whole ancient world from starvation and death. Pharaoh was afraid that the Israelites might become more numerous and more powerful than the Egyptians and decided to curb their progress and reduce their numbers. He attempted to have all the young males slaughtered and to obliterate or at least decimate Israel as a nation. The attempt to destroy Israel, which recurs again and again in history, started from a very early period. In this case, it is as though you find the prince of darkness standing behind Pharaoh on one hand while God is behind Moses on the other. Satan seeks to destroy not only Moses but all Israel, while God has ordained that through Israel the seed royal, Christ the Redeemer of the world, will ultimately be born. There behind natural men supernatural powers are in action. Battle is joined in the deep spiritual world, and is outworked in the natural world of men: the pieces fall into place for the great confrontation between good and evil and the ultimate deliverance of Israel.

As so often happens in a work of God, God chooses a man or a woman: He puts His hand upon one life. In this case He put His hand on Moses. At the same time, I imagine, Satan was stirring the heart of Pharaoh to obliterate Israel and to do it immediately. He was particularly minded to kill Moses, the future deliverer, the person who would typify the Christ Who was to come in later ages. Satan wanted Him destroyed right from birth and Satan's goal was not simply the destruction of a man or even of a race: it was the destruction of *the* race through which Christ was to be born. The action was against Christ Himself. In due time Moses was born of a Levite father and mother. The edict of the king had gone forth; he was to be put to death with all the other young male children of the same age. It is so similar to what happened when

Christ was born. Then Herod tried to destroy all the young males so that the Christ would also perish—but God![1]

Satan was minded to destroy Moses—but God intervened and the child was hidden by his mother in the bulrushes, discovered by Pharaoh's daughter, and brought up as her son. Events were turned upside down as God has such a wonderful way of doing; He altered circumstances and brought something forth for His own glory—He brought good out of evil.

In Egypt young Moses grew to manhood. He was carefully educated and was exceptionally intelligent, indeed head and shoulders, I imagine, above his peers. God wanted a deliverer—and you might say, 'Who better than this man?' With such a wonderful training, placed right next to Pharaoh's daughter, in line for the very throne of Egypt: what a wonderful position! Can you remember the temptation of Christ? 'I will give you all the kingdoms of the world if only you will fall down and worship me,' said Satan. A road to the throne that bypassed the cross, a totally forbidden road. In the case of Moses, too, a way seemed to be opening up for him to reach the throne and a position of tremendous influence which involved no cross. Ah, yes, Satan first tried to destroy him physically as an infant. Satan's next device seems to have been to destroy him spiritually by luring him into a wrong position in life which could have involved him in rejecting his own people. But God! But God! God had provided Pharaoh's daughter for his upbringing and Moses' own mother for his nurse. Through his mother he would imbibe the faith of the Hebrews very early and very deeply. His ultimate loyalty goes not to Pharaoh's daughter and to Egypt with all its paganism but to his own people and their God. The picture of a very energetic, able, strong young prince emerges: the early days of a man of destiny.

The day is to come when Moses will be described as the meekest man in all the earth, but Moses did not start by being a meek man at all. I want you—particularly leaders—to note what I say here very carefully. In choosing leaders, God, I suggest, very seldom if ever chooses 'wishy-washy' persons; the person who becomes a strong leader often starts by being an intolerable handful—quite intolerable. Be careful with the worst of the converts who come in—worst in the sense of being wilful, boisterous, full of life, mischief and energy. Do not despise them, because sometimes you are having the privilege of training the leaders of tomorrow. Always remember that. Moses may well have been an extremely turbulent, quick-tempered, violent, definite kind of character. Read carefully about his early life. He went out to have a look around him and came on a situation where an Egyptian was ill-treating an Israelite. No doubt the Egyptians were doing that left, right and centre, because by that time the Israelites were under cruel bondage, compelled to labour fantastic hours producing a fearful daily toll of bricks. They were being ill-treated, lashed and generally abused. But on this occasion Moses happened to come on abuse— and note his reaction. Did he say to the Egyptian, 'Now look, that's not fair, what you are doing: that's hard—you could be a bit kinder than that; you're hurting this fellow'? Nothing of the kind; he just killed him: he just took his life on the spot.

Moses, I think, was quite violent. You don't kill a man just like that if you haven't a violent potential in you. Next day he found two Israelites fighting and he would have separated them. He wasn't going to kill them: they were his brethren and brethren of each other; but the one who had wronged his neighbour said, 'Will you kill me the way you killed the Egyptian yesterday?' Moses realised that his earlier action was known and that his life was in danger, and he fled from Egypt to the land of Midian.... What does he do when he gets there? Is he a reformed character? Is he sorry he killed somebody? He's sitting at a well and seven young ladies are chased away from it by some shepherds. Moses doesn't just sit and look on; he gets up and chases the shepherds single-handed. He wasn't a weak man, but strong, powerful, determined. You may say, that would be the very kind of man God would want to work His works, but in fact it was not so. That man had to change; God had to break Moses. And a sore, sore breaking it would be. God changed Moses until he became the meekest man in all the earth, and through long years he led a murmuring people, and he led them skilfully and adroitly, wisely, kindly and lovingly.

Once in the later stages of his life we read of Moses losing his temper—for a moment—and that one mistake prevented his ever entering the land of promise.

You see, when you are an unbroken person and in training, it is amazing what God puts up with; but when you are called and chosen and know God deeply, one repetition of earlier mistakes can have disastrous consequences. It is as though in the training period God has infinite patience, but when you are where He wants you to be He puts great responsibility upon you and you dare not play the fool at that level of living.

Now God's hour has come to commission Moses to lead Israel out of Egypt. His first forty years have been lived in Egypt, the second forty in the back parts of the desert. Now, at eighty, his life-work is about to begin.

Note

[1] I often preach from these words, 'but God', having heard and been greatly impressed by a sermon of the late Dr Martin Lloyd Jones on the subject many years ago. It is amazing how often the phrase is used in relation to crisis hours throughout the Bible. Disastrous situation after disastrous situation is described and then we read the words, 'but God'. Divine intervention completely alters the course of events.

2

Holy Ground

Now Moses was keeping the flock of Jethro his father in law, the priest of Midian: and he led the flock to the back of the wilderness, and came to the mountain of God, unto Horeb. And the angel of the LORD appeared unto him in a flame of fire out of the midst of a bush: and he looked, and, behold, the bush burned with fire, and the bush was not consumed. And Moses said, I will turn aside now, and see this great sight, why the bush is not burnt. And when the LORD saw that he turned aside to see, God called unto him out of the midst of the bush, and said, Moses, Moses. And he said, Here am I. And he said, Draw not nigh hither: put off thy shoes from off thy feet, for the place whereon thou standest is holy ground. Moreover he said, I am the God of thy father, the God of Abraham, the God of Isaac, and the God of Jacob. And Moses hid his face; for he was afraid to look upon God (Ex 3:1–6).

This reading is of tremendous spiritual significance. We are not told much of what Moses did during the forty years in the back part of the desert. He would have time for reflection, time for meditation. In the New Testament we read that he chose the reproach of Christ rather than all the treasure of Egypt: rather than being counted the son of Pharaoh's daughter. This, I take it, happened before he fled from Egypt. In other words, the equivalent of a conversion experience happened in his unbroken early days. He appears to have been like so many of us who make our

24

choice for God but still remain wilful, determined, arrogant, opinionated, moving along lines of our own choosing. There for forty years Moses was given the opportunity to get to know God. He was in God's training school. That part may be regarded as the hidden years. We are told as little about Moses' inner communings as we are about those of Paul in a later day when he went into the aloneness before his public ministry started. I would love to have a diary of these years in both cases. I think that some of the most vital experiences in people's lives are never revealed: the formative years, the meditation, the drawing near of God to the soul, the drawing near of the soul to God, the communion, the getting to know God...like David the shepherd lad on the hillside who got to know God in the quietness and in the aloneness. Yes, he could deal with the lion and the bear out there alone on the mountainside, and with Goliath in front of the massed ranks of the Israelites and Philistines in battle array. This was no great matter to David, for by that time he knew God. He did not operate in the power of flesh and blood: he came against the giant in the name of the living God, and he prevailed.

We are not taken into all the innerness of the experiences of Moses in the back parts of the desert, but we come to the momentous hour when he saw the bush which burned with fire and was not consumed. You may say, 'What do you mean by *momentous hour*? We have been hearing about this hour all our lives in Christian circles. Why are you particularly pinpointing it?' It was then that Moses stood on holy ground and for every soul who knows such an hour the hour *is momentous*. Moses saw the burning bush and he saw that it burned and was not consumed: he saw that it was not just natural fire, which sometimes caused a bush to explode into flame in desert places. Such a bush catches fire and burns and is reduced to ashes, but here was one that was burning and was not being consumed. The fire that was burning was not natural fire but the fire of God, and Moses turned aside to see the wonder. Yes, he was attracted by the burning of the fire of God— every spiritual person is. Two people can come into a meeting in our own day, and one can react with fear and leave upset, while the other can feel the fire of God and be intensely attracted. When people adversely judge meetings where the power of God is present they frequently in fact pronounce judgment upon themselves. Those who are demon-troubled may run from a powerful service saying, 'It's terrible, terrible,' not realising that the demons in them are suffering fearfully because they have come near the fire of God. Their own condition is revealed in their reaction to the action of God. They often reveal in a moment of time the position in which they are.

Moses was attracted. 'Moses,' the voice sounds—the voice of God: 'put off thy shoes from off thy feet, for the place whereon thou standest is holy ground.' How would you have reacted? The human mind might say, 'It's not any different from any other bit of ground, it's just the sand of the desert: I'm not taking off my shoes, I'm not getting the sand between my toes!' Some people see nothing except sand, ordinary common or garden sand. The man of God, the spiritual man, however, doesn't see it that way. He is in touch with God, and he doesn't look at the ground at all. He doesn't look down; he just takes his shoes off right where he stands. This is not just a matter of the ground, it is the holiness of God: it is divine encounter: it is the divine presence that makes the ground holy. This is not just some unusual part of the desert. This is the revelation of the God of Israel to a chosen and prepared vessel, even to Moses— no longer, I suggest, the arrogant young man of forty years ago. I think the sandals came off promptly at the word of God. 'Don't come near here: don't come any further, for I am the God of thy father: I am the God of Abraham, Isaac and Jacob.' And so *Moses hid his face; for he was afraid to look upon God*, and God began to speak about the affliction of Israel and the fact that He had now come to deliver her. He then said, *Come now therefore, and I will send thee unto Pharaoh* (Ex 3:10).

'O God, I ran away from Egypt! I was afraid.' Yes, Moses, you ran away.

I believe the truth is this. From the beginning Moses was chosen of God to do the work of God for the deliverance of Israel, and Moses wanted to do that work in his own way. He took matters into his own hand, just the way you and I do with the work of God. 'We'll do it this way, we'll do it that way, we'll arrange this, and we'll arrange that. Lord, bless *my* work, put Thy stamp and Thy seal upon *my* work. O God...' and it is as if God says: 'Get out of my sight, it's time for you to get into the desert to learn wisdom, and when I bring you out of the desert *I* will tell you what to do, and you'll not tell *Me* what to do. Now, Moses, back you go to the place where you were your own man and acted in that way, and where you were ultimately scared to death and ran for your life: you get right back there.' Out of the belly of hell Jonah later cried and God delivered him, and God said, 'Now go right back to Nineveh, where I told you to go at first'—a chastened Jonah, bleached white, one would imagine, all the rest of his days!* Hard citizens, determined people, often run away from God, but God has His own ways of breaking them, and breaking them, and breaking them until they become useful to Him. Instead of living their own lives and doing their own thing they come under divine orders. In later days Moses is to be greatly used in leading Israel out of Egypt. He is to become one of the great leaders of all ages, and through it all God will never ask him for one opinion or suggestion of his own.

Let us jump forward for a moment. Moses was skilled in wisdom: head and shoulders above his fellows, and a day came when God wanted the tabernacle to be built and

---

* People who have come out of a shark or a great fish's belly are bleached totally white by the acids in the fish's stomach.

he took Moses and showed him His plan. He then said, 'Now see that you make it according to the plan that was shown you in the mount.' It was as though he took the very best of earth and he said, 'Now, Moses, you are skilled above all men—but I don't want one idea from you, I don't want one line, I don't want one plan, I don't want any fringe of a curtain, any shade of a colour, to be of your devising. You do the work exactly as I have shown you, absolutely and completely—don't alter or add anything: not one single idea of your own!'

Now I reiterate this and I emphasise it. Don't bring one idea into the work of God, not one idea: not the shade of an idea. God wants nothing to do with human ideas in His work.

> My hands were filled with many things
>   That I did precious hold
> As any treasure of a king's:
>   Silver, gems, or gold.
> The Master came and touched my hands:
> 'I must have empty hands,' said He,
> 'Wherewith to work my works through thee.'

Or again:

> Oh, the bitter shame and sorrow,
>   That a time could ever be,
> When I let the Saviour's pity
>   Plead in vain, and proudly answered,
> 'All of self, and none of Thee!'
>
> Yet He found me; I beheld Him
>   Bleeding on the accursed tree,
> Heard Him pray, 'Forgive them, Father!'
>   And my wistful heart said faintly—
> 'Some of self, and some of Thee.'
>
> Day by day His tender mercy,
>   Healing, helping, full, and free,

Sweet and strong, and, ah! so patient,
 Brought me lower, while I whispered,
'Less of self, and more of Thee.'

Higher than the highest heavens,
 Deeper than the deepest sea,
Lord, Thy love at last hath conquered;
 Grant me now my supplication—
'None of self, and all of Thee.'

Thomas Monod

I am not talking down to you. I have lots of ideas. All my life I've had ideas, and they come tumbling up and out and over. I have learned to be a bit more sensible in my later days. I let them bubble up and over and go down the drain-pipe. The revelation that comes from God and presents itself as an idea has something different about it. It has a fire in it. I can't always explain the difference, but there is something different. Have nothing to do with your own ideas. Tune in to what the Lord says. God's sentence is total death on all the carnal and merely human. God doesn't want it. He wants the divine springing up in the human, and moving through the human.

'Now, Moses. You are no longer a young fool; you are an older, wiser man—you go now and do what I tell you.'

And Moses said unto God, Behold, when I come unto the children of Israel, and shall say unto them, The God of your fathers hath sent me unto you; and they shall say to me, What is his name? what shall I say unto them? And God said unto Moses, I AM THAT I AM: and he said, Thus shalt thou say unto the children of Israel, I AM hath sent me unto you (Ex 3:13–14).

Moses asked a strange question, which led to a revelation about God not previously given. Asked for His Name, God said, *I AM THAT I AM*. God is the eternal self-existing One. 'Tell them,' He said, 'that I AM hath sent

thee. Tell them I am the God of Abraham, Isaac and
Jacob, and this is My Name for ever.'

> *And God said moreover unto Moses, Thus shalt thou say unto the
> children of Israel, The LORD, the God of your fathers, the God of
> Abraham, the God of Isaac, and the God of Jacob, hath sent me
> unto you: this is my name for ever, and this is my memorial unto all
> generations. Go, and gather the elders of Israel together, and say
> unto them, The LORD, the God of your fathers, the God of
> Abraham, of Isaac, and of Jacob, hath appeared unto me, saying,
> I have surely visited you, and seen that which is done to you in
> Egypt: And I have said, I will bring you up out of the affliction of
> Egypt unto the land of the Canaanite ... unto a land flowing with
> milk and honey. And they shall hearken to thy voice: and thou
> shalt come, thou and the elders of Israel, unto the king of Egypt,
> and ye shall say unto him, The LORD, the God of the Hebrews,
> hath met with us: and now let us go, we pray thee, three days'
> journey into the wilderness, that we may sacrifice to the LORD our
> God. And I know that the king of Egypt will not give you leave to
> go, no, not by a mighty hand. And I will put forth my hand, and
> smite Egypt with all my wonders which I will do in the midst
> thereof: and after that he will let you go* (Ex 3:15–20).

Now Moses was tough, very tough. 'In spite of what you
are telling me, Lord'—*they will not believe me, nor hearken
unto my voice: for they will say, The LORD hath not appeared
unto thee* (Ex 4:1).

I do not know whether the next incident, regarding
signs, would ever have happened if Moses had totally
believed God. I just do not know; but I suggest that
sometimes a sign is given to us not because of our great
faith but because of our lack of faith. Think of that for a
moment. You don't read much about signs with Abraham.
He believed God in the face of impossible circumstances.
He simply believed God. But here Moses has been speaking to God, and God to him, in wonderful intimacy—and
he suddenly turns round and says, 'But in spite of all that
they will not believe me.' In spite of what God says! Oh, a
bad man, Moses!—and we judge. Now, you who make

the judgment: what about you? In spite of all that God has done in your life, and the times he has met you wonderfully, is it not true that from time to time the very best of you don't believe God? There's no point in denying it: I have dealt with many at the very moment when they were not believing God in spite of all the wonderful things He had done in them. Unbelief had gripped the heart of Moses. Satan was moving in the background. Moses suddenly sees this vast company, this great nation, and sees himself going to tell them that God has sent him to deliver them from Pharaoh, and he says, 'They'll not believe me.' You can understand Moses: it's not difficult to empathise with him. If you stop thinking about God and think about the problem you empathise with Moses. If you think about God and His miraculous revelation to Moses and don't think about the vast number of the enslaved people, you think Moses is a fool. It depends which way you are looking. It depends on the picture you have. When Moses was looking Godward he would be all right, but when he looked manward he wouldn't be all right at all. His knees were shaking, he was scared stiff, and his faith fled. Like Peter on the water: when he looked at Christ all was well; when he looked at the waves, down he went. It's a repeated pattern in life. Moses had his objections, and God was very gracious at this point and very gentle.

He said, 'What is that in your hand?' As it happened, he had a rod in his hand. I don't suppose it would have mattered very much whether it had been a flask or a waterskin: God could have used anything that Moses had been carrying, but it happened to be a rod. God said, 'Throw it down,' and suddenly it became a serpent. 'Get it by the tail,' and it was a rod again—oh, wonderful, wonderful. This will catch them, this will impress them—and so it did.

'What if they still don't believe?'

'Well, put your hand in your bosom.' It comes out leprous.

'Put it in again,' and it comes out clean.

'What if they don't believe these two signs?'

'Pour water on the ground; see it turn to blood.'

You can almost see the fascination of the sensational and something of the unspirituality of the people to whom God is sending Moses. And unspirituality, you know, didn't die with the Israelites who were in Egypt. The sensational has a tremendous appeal to human nature, a tremendous appeal.

I have seen many miracles through the years— instantaneous healings, many deliverances from demons, and these have caused sensation. But, you know, some of the greatest miracles I have ever seen scarcely cause a ripple in many hearts. People could tell you how they were once in darkness and were then thoroughly converted and became lovers of God. This is an amazing miracle, a tremendous miracle. It's not sensational. It is different in kind from a body being healed in a moment of time; it doesn't have that particular quality, but it has another quality. A fallen son of Adam's race now follows Christ for love of Him.[1]

How do you think God evaluates these things? Do you think that healing of the body is more important than the salvation of the soul? In Christ's day some followed Him because of the loaves and the fishes, but there were others who followed Him for worthier motives, spiritual motives. Were the loaves and fishes for the feeding of the body more important than the teachings of Christ for the welfare of the soul? We are odd creatures and we make odd judgments.

Moses is given these mighty signs—and don't misunderstand, I don't downgrade these signs, not by a hairbreadth. I do not want you to get that impression, not for a moment. These were actions of the living God. But also remember the words of Christ: *An evil and adulterous generation seeketh after a sign* (Mat 12:39).

Note

[1] In recent years I have been increasingly involved in deliverance ministry. Many of the cases have been dramatic and indeed sensational, and the resulting testimonies make a deep impact on audiences. There is one kind of deliverance, however, which is less sensational than some others but is perhaps of much greater significance. The first type is from demon power—the latter from aspects of self. One of my own greatest conflicts with Satan in this ministry came on a night when a lady was set free from the power of her own stubborn will. She suddenly saw the ugliness of what she really was in this realm and realised her inability to be rid of it. She broke, and cried for mercy, and God wonderfully delivered her. She became a changed person. This was very quiet and had not the drama of certain bad cases of possession—but it may have been a much greater miracle. Deliverance from possession brings a person to a neutral position. Deliverance from self allows the Christ-nature to form in a life.

3

Resisting the Call

*And Moses said unto the LORD, Oh LORD, I am not eloquent,
neither heretofore, nor since thou hast spoken unto thy servant: for
I am slow of speech, and of a slow tongue. And the LORD said
unto him, Who hath made man's mouth? or who maketh a man
dumb, or deaf, or seeing, or blind? is it not I the LORD? Now
therefore go, and I will be with thy mouth, and teach thee what
thou shalt speak. And he said, Oh LORD, send, I pray thee, by the
hand of him whom thou wilt send. And the anger of the LORD was
kindled against Moses, and he said, Is there not Aaron thy brother
the Levite? I know that he can speak well. And also, behold, he
cometh forth to meet thee: and when he seeth thee, he will be glad
in his heart. And thou shalt speak unto him, and put the words in
his mouth: and I will be with thy mouth, and with his mouth, and
will teach you what ye shall do. And he shall be thy spokesman
unto the people: and it shall come to pass, that he shall be to thee a
mouth, and thou shalt be to him as God. And thou shalt take in
thine hand this rod, wherewith thou shalt do the signs (Ex 4:10–
17).*

Moses isn't finished with his opposition. He says to the
Lord: *I am not eloquent...for I am slow of speech, and of a
slow tongue.* There is real pathos in that verse. 'Lord, I am
not eloquent, I never was eloquent, and moreover, even
since You've spoken to me and I've had these dealings
with You, it hasn't changed that.'

34

You know, this is a great problem to some people who have deep encounter with God. There may be an area of their personality, or a physical condition, which after the encounter with God is over, after the baptism of the Spirit has come, after the call of God is received, is in no way altered. They suddenly realise that the former condition still remains. To some people this can be a tremendous disappointment. I personally was never a natural singer, and after my baptism in the Holy Spirit I was still not a natural singer. I can sing in the Spirit, but this has not changed me at a natural level at all. If you were good at mathematics before your encounter with God you are liable to remain good at mathematics, and if you were not good before it you are not apt to become good after it. This kind of spiritual experience does not necessarily touch those things. God, of course, can work a miracle in such areas, but it is not a likely or inevitable thing, and it is worth remembering that. Moses was of slow speech: he was not a good speaker either before or after his encounter with God. So we hear him say, 'I don't want to go: I am slow of speech, of a slow tongue,' and God says, *Who hath made man's mouth?* It seems almost as though God is saying: 'Moses, do you think I don't know about your speech difficulty? Don't you realise I have made you exactly as you are? Are you trying to suggest I have made a mistake in calling you?' Isn't this so often the attitude when we argue with God? In effect, we say, 'Lord, Lord, we don't agree.' What impertinence! One can understand people—they look into their own hearts and realise their own weakness and deficiency, and they say, 'Oh God, how can it be, how can it be?' I do not mind that attitude, but it is when they go beyond that and virtually accuse God of making a mistake that I feel the recoil. Sometimes the following lines are very apposite:

> How anxious is that man to go,
> Whom God hath never sent:

How timid, diffident and slow
God's chosen instrument.

God said, *Now therefore go, and I will be with thy mouth,
and teach thee what thou shalt speak*—and we come to the
crunch. The next verse is fearful: *Oh LORD, send, I pray
thee, by the hand of him whom thou wilt send*. And so God's
anger was kindled against Moses, and he said, 'Aaron is
eloquent, take him. He will be your spokesman. Take this
rod and do the signs.'

I am careful about what I say here, but I do suggest that
Aaron came into a position of prominence as a result of
this. One day Moses would come down Sinai from the
presence of God to find the people dancing around a
golden calf that Aaron had made: there would come a day
of rebellion in the camp and Aaron and Miriam would be
involved in it; Miriam would become a leper, white as
snow, as a result of the rebellion—and for all this Moses
may have been in one sense responsible. Had Aaron never
been involved in leadership, these events might never have
occurred. Always be extremely careful in the work of God:
never give a person a position that God doesn't give him or
her—never. The mistake is made again and again. God
often calls a person to do something and the first thing he
or she does is attempt to find somebody to carry the
responsibility, to come into the work with them, indeed to
share leadership. Never do that. Unless God shows you
clearly that someone is to be identified in leadership, never
open the door to it. Guard leadership, guard the call of
God.

People often come to me saying they feel a drive, a
desire to do something particular for God, and I nearly
always say to them, 'If God has given you a call and a
vision, get ahead with it.' Sometimes they will say, 'But I
would like so-and-so to take the lead and I would help
them.' I say, 'If God had wanted that person, don't you
think He would have called them? If God called *you*, *you*

do it: don't shuffle it on to somebody else who hasn't been given the call.' Oh, it can lead to tragedy when there are mistakes along this line—a God-given work can fail. Don't water down leadership, and also remember, there is no democracy with God—never, never.

So eventually Moses goes and does what he is told. The leaders gather, the signs are wrought, and the people believe when they hear that the Lord is visiting the children of Israel and has seen their affliction. They bow their heads and worship. Moses and Aaron go to Pharaoh and say, *Thus saith the LORD, the God of Israel, Let my people go, that they may hold a feast unto me in the wilderness* (Ex 5:1).

A further stage in the training of a deliverer, a man of God, has begun. From this first section there may be many parts that interest and appeal to you. There is one part that powerfully appeals to me: the moment when God said to Moses: *The place whereon thou standest is holy ground*. This is fascinating, profound, and of eternal significance. The words come winging down the ages and stir the appetite for such a moment—such moments change the lives of men and nations. Another dominant thought that has been in my mind is the greatness of God. I think there was instilled into the spirit of Moses something of this, and while I believe Satan struggled to discourage him by emphasising the difficulties and the problems, this was a counterbalance. After all the early skirmishing was over he would come back to the greatness of God. I AM THAT I AM, JEHOVAH, the eternal, self-existing One, the I AM, had commissioned him. As you go on with Moses through the ensuing years you feel you are in touch with a life that lives in the deeps of God. God goes with him and he goes with God. When a life comes into this position there is glory all around; because God is in action, miracles become normal occurrences.

4

Before Pharaoh

I have indicated a pattern that is found again and again in the Bible. God looked for deliverers and Satan attempted to destroy not only the individuals concerned, but the whole nation. Look at the juxtaposition of things in this case. God put His hand on Moses His champion, and Satan put his hand on Pharaoh. The contest took place in the spiritual world, but to a great extent was outworked in the natural world. This is not a solitary incident. There came a later time in the history of Israel when Satan was minded to obliterate the nation and moved Haman to fulfil his purposes. God used Mordecai and Esther to save them. God was interested not only in that generation but in the seed that would be born, in the Christ Who was to come through that nation. Satan, I imagine, having knowledge of that fact, was determined to destroy, to obliterate. In the case of Moses, Satan had plans for his destruction from early days, indeed from before his birth, as he had in a later day for the destruction of the Christ Himself, first at His birth, and later at Calvary.

Wonderful are the parallels. Again and again Satan moves and God moves to circumvent him. When David went down into the valley against Goliath with the sling and the five smooth stones, it may seem on the surface like a passing incident in history; but do you realise that the Christ would eventually be born of the line of David?— and there the stripling stands against the mighty giant of Gath. From one point of view it is as though the hope of all the ages was hanging on a very slender thread. What chance had David against Goliath? We know that there was no danger, for David's life was in God's hands; but from a human point of view the hour looked very, very dangerous for both David and his seed. You will find again and again in the history of Israel a recurrence of this kind of situation.

You may ask the question 'Why? Why does Satan do it?' and this is indeed an intriguing question. Beneath the surface of things there is regularly a moving of God and a counter-movement of Satan. Christ could say that before you destroy the strong man's goods you must first bind the strong man. As people grow into a spiritual maturity they begin to learn something of the spiritual warfare that lies in the unseen world. There is an outworking at surface levels, but deep below the surface there comes the spirit of intercession, there comes sharp contest with the powers of darkness, prior to the outflow of the blessing of God.

Recently I was in touch with a person who has been much used in the inner realm,* who said, 'You know, he came, Satan himself, and stood before me.' This happens from time to time in this lady's experience. God was minded to bless in a particular way and Satan himself came and stood before her to defy the Son of God, to prevent the outflow of blessing; if, in such an hour, God's servant goes under and fails to secure victory, neither will victory be experienced in the outward realm. This individual is now old and weakened in body but is still extremely potent in the service of God, and when she speaks of this kind of thing I always listen because of long years of experience of

* See Part 2 of the author's *A Trumpet Call to Women* (New Dawn Books, 1988). Since the above was written, this lady has gone home.

knowing the reality of her ministry. When Satan is moving
she becomes exceedingly sensitive, and I pay close attention to her warning. That Satan would prevent the blessing of God is not just theory that lies in Bible statements.
It is something that is real and up to date in our day. It is
so foolish to think that we will set the prisoners free
without the strong man being first bound. Our warfare is
not against flesh and blood, but against principalities and
powers, against spiritual wickedness in high and heavenly
places (see Eph 6:12).

So in the life of Moses we are past the early stages. He is
back in Egypt and the pieces are in place. He has been
very stubborn. He has almost refused to go. He has argued
with God, but ultimately he goes with Aaron to Pharaoh.
He is now a very different man from the man who earlier
in Egypt thought he could do God's work in his own way.
One day he killed an Egyptian in the strength of his
human might. A day is still future when he will no longer
use human might, yet Pharaoh and all his army will perish
in the sea by the action of God. Moses will be a deeply
changed person. He will depend no longer on human, but
on divine strength. In the name of the Lord he now goes
before Pharaoh.

The next part of this story is tremendous. We read of
the celebrated plagues of Egypt. They are fascinating and
sometimes horrific; they are unique in history. The first of
the signs are copied by the magicians, but there comes a
point when the magicians indicate that they can go no
further: they recognise the 'finger of God' and are stopped
in their tracks. Plague follows plague. Lice, frogs, locusts,
hail, and when the boils come on the people they come on
the magicians as well. God routs his enemies.

As you read, you may become intrigued with the phe-
nomena, and you may feel that Pharaoh was a fool. But
also realise that in Pharaoh there must have moved a
terrible, a devastating force. Time after time he seems to
be stripped and broken, broken almost to his knees as he

pleads with Moses to remove the plague of the hour, but as soon as the plague passes he changes his mind and will not let the people go. Exceedingly hard, exceedingly tough, exceedingly strong! This is the man whom God has sent Moses to deal with: the toughest man, I would imagine, in all the earth—and suddenly you realise that he is tough with a toughness that is not human. There is a power moving behind him, and there is a power moving through him that would defy the God of Israel; Satan has chosen his instrument well. And what does Moses do in the face of such an adversary?

This brings back to memory an experience of many years ago, when I was involved with someone regarding his baptism in the Spirit. This roused fearful fury in another person with whom I was very closely acquainted. In earlier days I had had many a contest with that person and in no way feared him, but when this arose I became conscious of darkness, danger, fearful strength of opposition, and for several months that darkness remained and I was never allowed to take any offensive action against the person who was bitterly attacking. I was not allowed to use any human instrument, or human weapon, to retaliate in kind, but had to endure suffering and pain. It was not easy to put aside offensive action in which the natural part might very much have liked to indulge. I waited, and suddenly one day something changed in the spiritual world and I had liberty to strike—I don't mean at a human level, not for a moment—but to strike spiritually and in the will of God. The tables were turned and the whole position reversed. Never from that hour had that particular person power over me.

Moses could not retaliate. The king had power, he had authority, he was the king, while Moses was the suppliant. Repeatedly Moses was dealt with deceitfully and promises were broken. Yet you never see a flash of uncontrolled anger: never a flash in the man who had slain the Egyptian in the power of his human strength in an earlier day. Now we see no hint of such reaction. It is as though he is under the covering of God, under the anointing of the divine: he is representing God and God alone; if God has something to say through him he says it, if God has nothing to say he keeps silent. He almost seems to stand outside the situation: he has committed the matter to God—he is there by divine choice and divine commission. He has nothing personally to do with the outworking of events. Moses is not himself the deliverer, Moses is the instrument of deliverance in the hand of God. Now let me say this to you. In your particular situation commit your cause to God, whatever your cause may be, and having committed it to Him never take it back into your own hand. Let Him deal with it totally and completely. You don't help a situation by reacting at a human level. You can be easily caught; fear can touch your spirit in a bad moment and you can play the fool in a dark moment, but as soon as you are back through to Christ don't allow any other consideration or person to exercise wrong influence. You are the servant of Christ, you are the servant of the living God. Commit everything to His hand and He will deliver you.

The Moses who goes back to Egypt is not the Moses who left Egypt: the new Moses is a man who knows God. It must have been exceedingly interesting to watch the developing situation from the sidelines. The wrath of Satan coming through the king, Pharaoh emanating hardness, cruelty, wickedness, sin, darkness, and Moses standing there unruffled, saying, *The God of the Hebrews hath met with us: let us go, we pray thee, three days' journey into the wilderness, and sacrifice unto the LORD our God* (Ex 5:3). Again and again there is request and rebuff and the warning that refusal will bring plague. Repeatedly plague comes crashing down on Pharaoh and the Egyptians. At times the king more or less screams for mercy, and then the whole process is repeated.

There is a strange word used. We read that Pharaoh hardened his heart, but we also read that God hardened it.

Woe betide the man or the woman who, on hardening the heart, finds that God hardens it. Something comes over such a person and he or she really hardens. Pharaoh's is an almost incredible story; the degree of the hardness is almost unbelievable. We need not go through all the details of the story, but a point comes where he says to Moses: *Get thee from me, take heed to thyself, see my face no more; for in the day thou seest my face thou shalt die* (Ex 10:28).

Pharaoh was enraged. He thoroughly lost his temper. He still did not realise how puny a little creature he was and how great was the God Whom he defied. Moses on the other hand, despite deep provocation and hot anger, maintained his serenity. Ever courteous, he courageously and firmly represented his God and carried out his commission. The man of God must never lose his temper (and to experience 'hot anger' does not imply this*). It is a most unwise thing to do. The wrath of man worketh not the righteousness of God, and the controlled course is not a soft option. Carnal weapons are very weak compared to spiritual weapons. Now Satan has a way of going too far and inviting defeat.[1] In his anger Pharaoh said, 'Get out of my sight—don't you appear before my face again or I will finish you!' Moses said, 'No, you won't see my face again, Pharaoh,' and little did Pharaoh realise the awfulness of that comment of Moses'. Pharaoh, you think you are going to finish this matter—the fact is, Pharaoh, that God is going to finish you. This brings us right up to the last plague, to the passover and the destruction of the firstborn of man and cattle, to the Exodus with the pursuing Egyptians, and the entanglement of the Israelites in the land with the sea before them and Pharaoh's host thundering up behind them to renew their enslavement.

---

*There is a righteous anger which is permissible.

Note

1   There is deep mystery in evil. Satan pushes things to extremes
    and we may often wonder why. Is it possible that there is a
    spiritual law which compels him so to do? Must evil forever
    express itself and perpetrate evil because it is evil—even to its
    own destruction? In this connection I recently came on the
    following fable, which puts this point very effectively.

> A scorpion, being a poor swimmer, asked a turtle to carry him
> on his back across a river.
>
> 'Are you mad?' exclaimed the turtle. 'You'll sting me while
> I'm swimmming and I'll drown!'
>
> 'My dear turtle,' laughed the scorpion, 'if I were to sting you,
> you would drown and I would go down with you! Now, where is
> the logic in that?'
>
> 'You're right!' cried the turtle. 'Hop on!'
>
> The scorpion climbed aboard and, half-way across the river
> gave the turtle a mighty sting. As they both sank to the bottom,
> the turtle resignedly said, 'Do you mind if I ask you something?
> You said there'd be no logic in your stinging me. Why did you do
> it?'
>
> 'It had nothing to do with logic,' the drowning scorpion
> replied, sadly. 'It's just my character.'

From Stephen Gaukroger and Nick Mercer, *Frogs in Cream*
(Scripture Union, 1990), p.40.

We may smile, but a serious point is made.

Take the mystery of the cross. Satan strove to have Christ
nailed to that tree and yet it is from that tree that life flows to
all mankind. To the very cross which in a sense Satan himself
erected, all the ages look. Surely God brought glorious good
from heinous evil. And is it not that same cross which seals
Satan's own final destiny?

For ever Satan goes too far and for this I have often been
thankful. Frequently temptation may at first appear to be
innocent. As an angel of light the wicked one comes, but if
you have patience and don't rush to fulfil the first desire, you
will notice that gradually he is forced to reveal himself.
Ultimately his true colours show—the cloven hoof emerges.
Have you ever pondered what I would almost name the
impertinence of the last temptation of Christ in the wilderness—the idea that the Son of God, the Holy One, should
actually bow down and worship Satan? The pride and

arrogance of it is breathtaking—but it shows how far Satan will go and how his identity ultimately becomes apparent. The angel of light turns to a horrible ugliness at the last.

5

*The Passover**

First, let us look at the passover.

Throughout the Old and New Testaments blood is extremely significant. Back in Eden, man in his nakedness would have covered his shame with fig leaves. God, instead, gave him a covering that required the shedding of blood. An animal had to die. Right from the earliest day it was clear that there was no covering for sin that did not involve the shedding of blood. Soon Cain and Abel, the first men born, were to approach God. Cain offered the fruit of the cursed earth and his offering was rejected. Abel came by blood sacrifice, and this was acceptable to God. In a later day when the law was given and priestly service regulated there was very particular emphasis on the offering of animals and the shedding of their blood. We learn later that these sacrifices pointed to the sacrifice of the Christ Who was to come and to the shedding of His blood. Salvation was to be offered to the world on the ground of that sacrifice of inestimable worth. That blood was to atone for all our sin. We read, *All we like sheep have gone astray; we have turned every one to his own way; and the*

* This chapter is taken, with minor adjustments, from chap. 6 of the author's *Gospel Vignettes* (New Dawn Books, 1989).

46

LORD *hath laid on him the iniquity of us all* (Isa 53:6). The Lamb of God was to die. The writer of the book of Hebrews could later say, *And according to the law, I may almost say, all things are cleansed with blood, and apart from shedding of blood there is no remission* [i.e., of sins] (Heb 9:22), and John wrote, *The blood of Jesus his Son cleanseth us from all sin* (1 Jn 1:7). As the poet could write: 'The blood has always precious been.' Indeed, the Bible teaches that the life is in the blood, and Christ gave this on Calvary as a sacrifice for sin.

Before these truths were revealed, the passover took place. God instructed Moses to have the Israelites take lambs and at a given time slay them and with hyssop sprinkle their blood on the doorposts and lintels of their houses. The flesh they were to roast and eat. They were to eat in haste as people going on a journey. At the midnight hour a destroying angel would pass through the land of Egypt killing all the firstborn of men and cattle who were not in houses marked with blood.

> For I will go through the land of Egypt in that night, and will smite all the firstborn in the land of Egypt, both man and beast; and against all the gods of Egypt I will execute judgements: I am the LORD. And the blood shall be to you for a token upon the houses where ye are: and when I see the blood, I will pass over you, and there shall no plague be upon you to destroy you, when I smite the land of Egypt (Ex 12:12–13).

When I see the blood I will pass over you. It happened exactly as predicted:

> And it came to pass at midnight, that the LORD smote all the firstborn in the land of Egypt, from the firstborn of Pharaoh that sat on his throne unto the firstborn of the captive that was in the dungeon; and all the firstborn of cattle. And Pharaoh rose up in the night, he, and all his servants, and all the Egyptians; and there was a great cry in Egypt; for there was not a house where there was not one dead (Ex 12:29–30).

Shall we stand back and see the picture? Put yourself in the place of a young Israelite and a young Egyptian on that momentous night in Egypt—a night which was to be commemorated in Israel as the feast of the passover through all later generations.

I can imagine the Egyptian jeering, if indeed word of what was afoot reached his ears. 'Why are you putting blood on your doorposts and lintels? It is unsightly and distasteful.'

'Because Moses has warned us that at midnight we must be in our houses and under the sign of blood, for then a destroying angel will pass over and slay all the firstborn.'

'But what has blood got to do with it? Why, at midnight, blood will be invisible. If you want your houses to be identified surely light-coloured paint or whitewash would be more suitable.'

'No! Moses said we were to sprinkle blood.'

'Why, the whole thing is ridiculous. There is no record in history of this, or anything like it, ever happening before. I just do not believe it. Your religion is phoney. You think you will escape us and go with Moses into the wilderness. I tell you Pharaoh will never allow it. You are our slaves for ever. See if your faith in the blood of a lamb will do you the slightest good.'

We can understand that the godless Egyptian might have jeered, although in the light of past plagues and miracles one might have expected him to be at least circumspect and cautious, even if not wholly believing. We have no record that any of the Egyptians sought entrance to a blood-stained home or escaped the judgment.

With a young Hebrew we could expect things to be different. He would have a knowledge of God, as a result of his upbringing, but no doubt there were great differences between individuals. I imagine that the more conservative of them would give unquestioning heed to the words of Moses and resolve to be under the blood at the critical hour. Others might have been foolishly daring and been tempted to be out on the kind of concerns that occupied the 'fast set' of that day—if there was such an equivalent to our day. You can imagine many a person cogitating about various aspects of Moses' instructions and especially about the significance of the blood. I imagine that to most it would be a total mystery whose full significance was understood neither then nor later. Many would make sure of being in their dwellings at the critical hour, simply on the word of Moses and not because they understood why a destroying angel would spare the houses marked with blood. God did not enlighten His people at that time and indeed we do not know that Moses himself fully understood the significance of the celebration for which he gave such clear instruction or precisely what it foreshadowed.

We who live in a later day have a fuller understanding. There came another momentous night on earth when the Lamb of God, foreshadowed in the passover lamb, was slain. His blood too was shed, and God has given the assurance that all who come under its covering will be safe from coming destruction. There is an hour of holocaust ordained. There is a midnight hour for the world, and death, eternal death, is the fate of all who are not under the blood.

There are many in our day, even amongst religious leaders, who hate what they call this blood religion. Infamously and blasphemously they sometimes refer to it as a slaughterhouse religion. The idea of the need for blood sacrifice is resisted—but the teaching of the Bible is unambiguous; cleansing and forgiveness of sin come through the blood of Christ. He gave His own blood as an offering for sin. The life was in the blood and this He gave for men. The Bible makes it quite clear that there is no other way of acceptance. The blood is applied when the soul yields to Christ. Its atoning efficacy is imparted: *and when I see the blood, I will pass over you.* The words forever apply—there is no other place of safety as we go out into eternity. The provision is made. But as with the Hebrews of old, it must be applied and, as with them, we must forever remain under its covering.

The accuracy of the foreshadowing is remarkable. At the appointed anniversary of the passover Christ died. *He* was the passover lamb. *He* was our passover slain for us.[1] Through His death a safe covering was found for men. His shed blood saves from a greater destruction than Egypt ever knew. As it was essential for men to be under the covering then, so is it necessary now.

May I ask the question pointedly: 'Have you come in?' So many, it seems to me, have substituted whitewash for blood—good works, fair in the sight of men, indeed eye-catching: likely to be seen by men and angels. Is this not a better hope than the blood of another? In Egypt, white doors might have been expected to be more visible than doors stained with blood. But it was over the latter that the destroying angel passed without dealing death. There was no safety in the former.

In the matter of your soul's welfare you cannot afford to make mistakes. Even if you don't fully understand the significance of blood any more than the Israelites did, still come under the shelter. He saves many a soul who never fully plumbs the depths of Calvary or understands all its significance. Indeed, who amongst us ever can fully plumb those depths or ever fully know their significance this side of eternity? And perchance not even then shall we know all.

In Egypt, on that night long ago there came an eleventh and then a midnight hour. As the angel destroyed in Egypt, so there is coming an hour of judgment on the world. As men required the covering of blood then, so do we now. There is no other safe shelter. Many of us feel that we are already in the eleventh hour, with midnight fast approaching. It is time to be fully prepared.

Christ so clearly portrayed the fate of the unprepared soul in a pointed parable. For the wedding feast of a king's son, wedding-garments were prepared for guests and were obligatory. There came in a man not having a wedding-garment but clothed in his own robes. *Friend,* said the Master, *how camest thou in hither not having a wedding-garment?* Without a word to say in his own defence the man is cast into the outer darkness where, we read, *there shall be the weeping and gnashing of teeth.* No doubt he had thought his own raiment perfectly adequate but it did not suffice in that hour. Like many another he probably depended on his own good works and was proud of his own self-righteous garments, forgetting that God has said that *all our righteousness is as filthy rags.* As one has poetically expressed it, 'The only garment that avails in that hour was woven on the looms of Calvary.' It is the garment of salvation, and as surely as blood had to be shed to provide our first parents' coverings, so did the blood of God's Son have to be shed to provide this salvation.

And when I see the blood I will pass over you.

Note

[1] Even as Christ died, a vast number of lambs were being slain in Jerusalem. These, according to the law, were to be without blemish. Christ, the Sinless One, is our paschal Lamb.

6

Deliverance with a Mighty Hand

And the LORD spake unto Moses, saying, Speak unto the children
of Israel, that they turn back and encamp before Pi-hahiroth,
between Migdol and the sea, before Baal-zephon: over against it
shall ye encamp by the sea. And Pharaoh will say of the children
of Israel, They are entangled in the land, the wilderness hath shut
them in (Ex 14:1–3).

And the LORD hardened the heart of Pharaoh king of Egypt, and
he pursued after the children of Israel: for the children of Israel
went out with an high hand. And the Egyptians pursued after
them, all the horses and chariots of Pharaoh, and his horsemen,
and his army, and overtook them encamping by the sea, beside Pi-
hahiroth, before Baal-zephon. And when Pharaoh drew nigh, the
children of Israel lifted up their eyes, and, behold, the Egyptians
marched after them; and they were sore afraid; and the children of
Israel cried out unto the LORD. And they said unto Moses,
Because there were no graves in Egypt, hast thou taken us away to
die in the wilderness? wherefore hast thou dealt thus with us, to
bring us forth out of Egypt? (vv.8–11).

And Moses said unto the people, Fear ye not, stand still, and see
the salvation of the LORD, which he will work for you to-day: for
the Egyptians whom ye have seen today, ye shall see them again no
more for ever. The LORD shall fight for you, and ye shall hold your
peace.

And the LORD said unto Moses, Wherefore criest thou unto me? speak unto the children of Israel, that they go forward. And lift thou up thy rod, and stretch out thine hand over the sea, and divide it: and the children of Israel shall go into the midst of the sea on dry ground (vv.13–16).

And Moses stretched out his hand over the sea; and the LORD caused the sea to go back by a strong east wind all the night, and made the sea dry land, and the waters were divided. And the children of Israel went into the midst of the sea upon the dry ground: and the waters were a wall unto them on their right hand, and on their left. And the Egyptians pursued, and went in after them into the midst of the sea, all Pharaoh's horses, his chariots, and his horsemen (vv.21–3).

And the Lord said unto Moses, Stretch out thine hand over the sea, that the waters may come again upon the Egyptians, upon their chariots, and upon their horsemen. And Moses stretched forth his hand over the sea, and the sea returned to its strength when the morning appeared; and the Egyptians fled against it; and the LORD overthrew the Egyptians in the midst of the sea. And the waters returned, and covered the chariots, and the horsemen, even all the host of Pharaoh that went in after them into the sea; there remained not so much as one of them (vv.26–8).

And Israel saw the great work which the LORD did upon the Egyptians, and the people feared the LORD: and they believed in the LORD, and in his servant Moses (v.31).

Have you ever realised that while Israel wandered for forty years in the desert the journey between Egypt and Israel could have been accomplished in a few days? God deliberately led them into the wilderness. As one has said, 'It was more difficult to get Egypt out of Israel than it was to get Israel out of Egypt,' and in the wilderness God dealt with them for their good. They were given the law and preliminary training, but they were slow to learn and proved to be stiff-necked and rebellious. They resisted the training and reaped the consequences. Apart from Joshua and Caleb the whole generation which left Egypt perished in the wilderness, and the people who ultimately went into the land of promise had some knowledge of the living God.

Note that at this particular point God said, 'Go back.' They were going one way in their escape from Egypt; they had a reasonable start and could probably have been well beyond the easy reach of Pharaoh. God deliberately turned them back and He turned them back into a strait place, a hard place where they were entangled in the land. The sea was before them, and the configuration of land behind them was such that there was no way of escape from a pursuing army. God brought them into these circumstances deliberately. It was the will of God that they should be in these dire straits, so that the purposes of God might be outworked—and one of the purposes of God, we are clearly told, was the bringing of judgment on Pharaoh. It was in God's deliberate plan that a final judgment should come upon Satan's emissary and his hosts. Israel too was to go through an experience which would show her something of the greatness of God. She had seen miracle after miracle in Egypt. There she had been downtrodden and under cruel bondage, but basically her continued existence was not in danger. Though she had known intense suffering, wholesale genocide was not threatened.[1] But now there seems to be a danger of fearful destruction either from the unparting sea or from the vast host of Pharaoh thundering up behind with great chariots. Although Pharaoh's declared objective was to bring Israel back into slavery, the fleeing people did not know this, and to them there seemed to be a real danger of death.

I think this is the most dreadful hour in Israel's history up to this point—the darkest hour, the most dangerous hour. No way through, no way back: circumstances hemming the people in. Think of the position of Moses. Read carefully and you will realise that God had spoken to Moses of what would ensue. But we are not told in this case how God spoke. There are times when He speaks to you and to me and we know His voice, and not long after

we have heard it Satan says, 'Now are you quite sure that
was God speaking? Was it not just your imagination? How
do you know for certain it was the voice of God?' We are
not told here how Moses knew, and I suggest there may
have come a moment when he saw the waters before him
and the pursuing host behind and realised that in one
sense he was responsible for hundreds of thousands of
Israelites who had trusted him and whom he had led from
Egypt. The people were absolutely petrified; they were
unarmed and afraid, and said to Moses, 'Are there no
graves in Egypt, that you brought us out here to die in the
wilderness?' They had no faith in God, and Moses stood
between as God's man. Friends, the darkest hour is frequently before the dawn, and there comes in the lives of
men and women of God an hour of testing which is the
darkest time in all their lives. There comes a time which if
successfully gone through leads to a new place with God,
and those who do go through it may live in the power of
the victory of the Lord Jesus Christ.

My mind reaches backward to a number of men and
women of old. Come with me for a brief moment.

I suggest there was an hour in Abraham's life that was
different from every other hour—it was that hour when
God said, *Take now thy son, thine only son, whom thou
lovest, even Isaac, and get thee into the land of Moriah; and
offer him there for a burnt offering upon one of the mountains
which I will tell thee of* (Gen 22:2). Now I believe that God
previously spoke to Abraham. I believe that Abraham
himself believed that through that son all the nations of the
earth would be blessed, and that they would be blessed
through that boy even if it meant the death of Isaac and
God's raising him from the dead—but even so there came
for Abraham an hour when not only in spirit but in physical fact he went up that lonely mountain with the lad, a
lad enquiring as to the sacrifice: 'Here is the wood, here is
the fire, for the burnt offering; but where is the lamb?'—
God will provide Himself a lamb—and the awful hour

came when Abraham bound his son to that altar. He actually raised the sacrificial knife to plunge it into his son before God stayed his hand and provided a lamb. Now I am not aware of any greater test that Abraham had to meet in all his later life. There seems to come a high point in a life in this kind of thing.

Consider Jacob. Jacob had a rough life—maybe partly of his own making. But there came an hour when at the command of God he went back into the land of his fathers, knowing that he would meet Esau whom he had so grievously offended. He was a planner, was Jacob, and he sent his goods on before him, flock after flock with spaces between; and he himself abode all night on the near side of the brook Jabok. That night there came an angel and wrestled with him until the breaking of day. Jacob was terrified of his brother, and with reason. Jacob had to know God. Jacob had to overcome, and he overcame, and he found a new place with God. He went over to victory.

Turn now to the life of Joseph.

Oh, yes, he had his hard times. He knew what it was to be down the pit and have his coat of many colours sent to his father with the story that a wild beast had devoured him. He knew what it was to be sold into Egypt as a slave. He knew what it was to be wrongly accused by Potiphar's wife and imprisoned for long years. It seems not unreasonable to imagine that there would come a high point of crisis, perhaps after the butler and the baker had their dreams interpreted and went out, the butler to be reinstated and the baker to be hanged on a tree. The butler forgot his debt and his promise to Joseph, who was left languishing there in the inmost prison. We read that iron entered into his soul. I believe there came a critical point—a high point in testing.

Go through the lives of many of the Bible characters, and you will find that there frequently came a fearful hour. Think of Shadrach, Meshach and Abednego. Can you think of anything more severe than going into the middle of that burning fiery furnace? There were many conflicts in Daniel's life, many tests, but do you think there was ever any greater than being thrown to the lions? Actually envisage it—it's too easy to be casual and calmly objective—but you are Daniel, and you have done your duty: you have obeyed the law of God, you have refused to worship the golden image, and the hour comes when they take you to the lions' den. They are all there and they're hungry. They are not chained. The moment comes when you go tumbling down into the midst of the den. What was Daniel thinking about? What was he feeling? What were his sensations? You know, at the end of the night I'm sorrier for the lions than I am for Daniel. What frustration! They can't lay a paw on him. They couldn't get a bite at him the whole night long. He's in the protection of the living God. I doubt if Daniel was ever tested in quite that way or to quite that degree again.

I wonder about Paul. Paul was lashed five times with thirty-nine stripes, shipwrecked, pursued by bandits— about forty people who had bound themselves with a fearful curse neither to eat nor drink until they had taken his life: all that kind of thing. That was fairly normal for Paul—par for the course, as the saying goes. But, you know, they really went past it one time—and again I ask you to try to enter into it, not just think about it. You're Paul, and they've really gone over the top this time, and they are having no more of you. They've got you outside the city gate and they're stoning you with stones. You feel the first of these as they land on you; the normal thing with the professional stone throwers was to throw in such a way as to break both arms so that you couldn't defend your face, and then just gradually kill you. They left Paul for dead—they killed him, or so they thought. He went down under the rain of missiles like a dead body. We read later that Paul said (possibly concerning himself),

I know a man in Christ (whether in the body, I know not; or

whether out of the body, I know not; God knoweth), such a one caught up even to the third heaven. And I know such a man (whether in the body, or apart from the body, I know not; God knoweth), How that he was caught up into Paradise, and heard unspeakable words, which it is not lawful for a man to utter (2 Cor 12:2–4).

Paul was a terrible man. What could you do with a man like this? You kill him and he goes into glory, and after he's had his wonderful trip of ecstasy he comes back into his body and gets up and walks away—not only does he walk away, but he goes on preaching. He doesn't turn aside for a moment: a man of God.

In all of these cases I think you could have understood and had a certain amount of sympathy if they had failed: if Abraham, for example, had said, 'I'm sorry, I can't go this far. I really can't kill my son.'

'Well, Abraham, I can understand that,' we would say.

If Jacob had said to God, 'Well, yes, but I know Esau. I've known Esau from my earliest days and Esau will kill me. I'm sorry, I'm not going over that brook. I'm sorry, Lord, but I just can't do it.'

I think you could have understood if Joseph had said, 'I've had enough. I've had wonderful visions. I saw the sun and the moon and the stars bow down, and I saw the sheaves bow down, and I knew that there were great things ahead in the economy of God; but the fact of the matter is, I've been down in the dungeon and now I'm in jail...I've been in jail for years and now it's getting worse, and nobody remembers me. The iron is not only on my limbs, it's in my soul, and I'm finished. I've had enough.'

People would have understood.

If Shadrach, Meshach and Abednego had said, 'Well, Lord, we were prepared to follow you. We were prepared to live for you, Lord, but you know we never realised it would mean going into a burning fiery furnace seven-times heated.'

We could have said, 'Well, Shadrach, I understand

that. I don't know that I'd have been able to go in there—indeed, even thinking about it scares me stiff, especially as I realise that when you saw the flames you didn't know then that you would see and walk with Christ in the midst of the flames.' We could have understood his turning aside.

And if we had stood with Daniel and seen the gnashing teeth of these great creatures and had heard him say, 'Well, I'm sorry, it's too much,' we might not have condoned but at least we would have understood. If Paul had said, 'I don't want to die this cruel death, Lord—have I not been through enough? They've been trying to kill me now for years. I'm tired, Lord. I can't go through any more,' we would have understood. When he did come back to health, if he had said, 'Lord, there are a lot of other people in the church: there are younger men. Lord, why me?' we might have been disappointed, but we would have understood.

God allows horrendous circumstances to come into the lives of men and women whom he wants to place in the highest spiritual places—not for their sakes but for His own glory. If you are peculiarly tried, you are peculiarly favoured. If you are lightly tried, you are perchance lightly favoured. What an honour to stand with these giants of old and be tested and trusted—trusted as Job was trusted. Can you think of the tragedy if Moses had said, 'Lord, I'm sorry. I know you've been with me through all the plagues in Egypt, but this is too much. How can I go through there? I can't walk on the water. I can't walk back through these chariots. I'm absolutely stuck, Lord.' The man who had initially said, 'Send by whom you will send, but don't send me,' you might have expected to crack—to say, 'Lord, I'm through.' Oh, the shame of Israel, discomfited in the eyes of the nations. But God had put his iron in Moses and Moses obeyed the Living God. God said, 'What are you talking to me for? Talk to the people, that they go forward.' (God had told them earlier to go backward—

backward into the problem. Now He tells them to go forward—forward through the problem.) 'The time for talking to Me is over. Be my mouthpiece and lead them over. Speak to the people that they go forward.'

It's my job to speak to people in their darkest hours, that they go forward. I'm not through yet on this subject. There is one life that we haven't looked at, one situation that we haven't observed: the life and death of the Lord Jesus Himself.

I think there would be little controversy about the darkest hour—the time that came very soon before and at the cross: Gethsemane and Calvary. The awful darkness of these hours! He stood at a place that none of these other heroes of faith ever knew. Tested as they were, no one of them was tested as the Lord Jesus was tested. Shadrach, Meshach and Abednego, and Daniel: their bodies seemed to be in desperate danger—but in Christ's case, the burden of a world came upon Him. He was out in a spiritual dimension, knowing the horrors of approaching hell and the darkness of Satan all around Him. He was in a spiritual dimension far beyond and above body, and the pain and the racking and the agony of Calvary were but an outworking of a darker, deeper agony—the Son of God! There was never another hour and never will be, through all eternity, in which He went or will go through that or anything like it again. There came a crescendo and a change for ever. I want you to notice another thing. In Christ's case, He was within hours of the glory of resurrection and the outflowing of the floods of eternal life to mankind. The darkest hour before the dawn: the cross and crucifixion before resurrection. In the case of Joseph, he was about to become the deliverer of Egypt, the most powerful man next to Pharaoh in the whole kingdom, the saviour of the ancient world—down in a dark dungeon, out into the light of a new day. And you will find it is repeated again and again. In the case of Moses, the dark, the difficulty, the danger, of that hour, and the sudden reversal: the incoming floods of water that destroyed the enemy in the midst of the sea while Moses went over on dry land and led his people toward their promised land. Child of God, be careful. One able writer once said, 'When God is about to make princes of us we make fools of ourselves.' We often meet the deep test on the threshold of the gates of glory, and if we fail we are unable to grasp the coming opportunity: we are weak in the day of God's power. If, however, we hang on and allow God to hang on to us, we go through to victory and overcoming and glory. Blessed be the name of the Lord.

Note

1 Pharaoh's unsuccessful attempt to have all Hebrew boys slaughtered at birth (Ex 1:15–22) seems to have been with a view to the decimation, rather than total extermination, of the Israelites.

7

Preservation through Intercession

Then came Amalek, and fought with Israel in Rephidim. And Moses said unto Joshua, Choose us out men, and go out, fight with Amalek: to-morrow I will stand on the top of the hill with the rod of God in mine hand. So Joshua did as Moses had said to him, and fought with Amalek: and Moses, Aaron, and Hur went up to the top of the hill. And it came to pass, when Moses held up his hand, that Israel prevailed; and when he let down his hand, Amalek prevailed. But Moses' hands were heavy; and they took a stone, and put it under him, and he sat thereon; and Aaron and Hur stayed up his hands, the one on the one side, and the other on the other side; and his hands were steady until the going down of the sun. And Joshua discomfited Amalek and his people with the edge of the sword. And the LORD said unto Moses, Write this for a memorial in a book, and rehearse it in the ears of Joshua: that I will utterly blot out the remembrance of Amalek from under heaven (Ex 17:8–14).

And the LORD spake unto Moses, Go, get thee down; for thy people, which thou broughtest up out of the land of Egypt, have corrupted themselves: They have turned aside quickly out of the way which I commanded them: they have made them a molten calf, and have worshipped it, and have sacrificed unto it, and said, These be thy gods, O Israel, which brought thee up out of the land of Egypt. And the LORD said unto Moses, I have seen this people, and, behold, it is a stiffnecked people: Now therefore let me alone, that my wrath may wax hot against them, and that I

*may consume them: and I will make of thee a great nation. And
Moses besought the LORD his God, and said, LORD, why doth thy
wrath wax hot against thy people, which thou hast brought forth
out of the land of Egypt with great power and with a mighty hand?
Wherefore should the Egyptians speak, saying, For evil did he
bring them forth, to slay them in the mountains, and to consume
them from the face of the earth? Turn from thy fierce wrath, and
repent of this evil against thy people. Remember Abraham, Isaac,
and Israel, thy servants, to whom thou swarest by thine own self,
and saidst unto them, I will multiply your seed as the stars of
heaven, and all this land that I have spoken of will I give unto
your seed, and they shall inherit it for ever. And the LORD
repented of the evil which he said he would do unto his people* (Ex
32:7–14).

*And Moses returned unto the LORD, and said, Oh, this people
have sinned a great sin, and have made them gods of gold. Yet
now, if thou wilt forgive their sin—; and if not, blot me, I pray
thee, out of thy book which thou hast written. And the LORD said
unto Moses, Whosoever hath sinned against me, him will I blot out
of my book* (vv. 31–3).

Were I asking you wherein you think the greatness of
Moses as a man of God is most supremely exemplified, I
think you might say: as a lawgiver, a statesman, a leader, a
great mystic, a miracle worker. He was indeed all of these
things—a man greatly gifted and deeply called—but
there was perhaps one area in which he excelled: the realm
of intercession.

Very soon after coming into the wilderness Israel was
attacked by Amalek, and during the ensuing battle Moses
was on the hilltop in intercession for the nation. While his
hands were raised to God, Israel prevailed; when his hands
went down, Amalek prevailed. When he was too weary to
hold his arms up, Aaron on one hand and Hur on the other
gave support until the victory was won.

Here we see Moses as an intercessor. He had power
with God and with man. Here was a man to whom God
hearkened, a man who prayed according to the will of

God, a man through whom God's power flowed. Moses was an intercessor, and an effective intercessor.

A deeper and more desperate conflict was to follow. On the mountain top God spoke to Moses face to face—at the foot of the mountain Israel sinned grievously. The people feared, or perchance hoped, that Moses was dead (they had heard and perhaps been appalled at the ten commandments and the law which had already been declared to them). Moses had been away for a long time, and in spite of having heard the ten commandments earlier they actually turned to idolatry. Aaron was persuaded to make a golden calf for which they generously contributed their gold and which they were delighted to worship. *These* (they said) *be thy gods, O Israel, which brought thee up out of the land of Egypt* (Ex 32:4).

> *And when Aaron saw this, he built an altar before it; and Aaron made proclamation, and said, To-morrow shall be a feast to the* LORD. *And they rose up early on the morrow, and offered burnt offerings, and brought peace offerings; and the people sat down to eat and to drink, and rose up to play* (vv. 5–6).

I do not want to go into detail about these background events, but I ask you to observe that in the very midst of idolatry Israel paid lip-service and sacrificed to the living God. Aaron did not want to leave God out of things, but he was not prepared to take an uncompromising stand for God: he wanted to stand well with both God and the idolaters—and this just could not be done. Neither then nor now is this acceptable to God—although many in our day still try it. With great strength Moses, a sterling leader, on coming down from the mountain, broke the calf in pieces and, under God, broke the whole rebellion.

And now to the point. I want you to see Moses in what was perhaps his greatest ministry. He had delivered a people under God, and yet because of her rebellion and idolatry Israel was on the brink of destruction. Under God Moses became her preserver. A people delivered from bondage was now preserved through intercession. Again, I want you to think—not just to read casually, but actually to think. The nation is on the brink of being blotted out and Moses has a burden for the people. They have not been very grateful for all he has done for them—indeed, they have been positively objectionable—but he loves his nation and he loves his God; moreover, he is jealous for the honour of God and most anxious lest the heathen rejoice and accuse the God of Israel of bringing the nation out of Egypt to slay them in the mountain.

I believe God tested Moses, and when God tests you He doesn't always, if ever, say, 'Now I'm giving you a test.' You are not always aware that you are being tested. I suggest that God tested Moses to the very roots of his being. He said to him, *I will make of thee a great nation.* You see, God could still fulfil his promise to Abraham, Isaac and Jacob, and raise up descendants through Moses. What an honour, or seeming honour, was presented to Moses! He would go down in history as an almost unique person—a progenitor of Israel. How many would have resisted such an honour then, or some kind of unique distinction now? There are so many people amongst Christians who are out, at least in a measure, for themselves—for what they can get out of a situation. How they would love to be great, to be well known, to be famous, to be successful, to have a very important role.

'Moses, here is perhaps the most important role on earth that you could be offered. Moses, Israel deserves to be punished, to be blotted out, and you can honourably take what God is holding out to you.'

But Moses loved the people. Moses loved the people more than he loved himself, more than he wanted a great name of his own. In a later day Paul took a similar line, actually saying that he could almost wish himself anathema—away from Christ altogether—if thereby it would mean the salvation of his people. He loved his people to the extent that he seems to have been prepared, or almost prepared, to forfeit his own salvation if thereby it would be the means of saving them. Moses said, 'Blot my name out. Blot my name out—but, Lord, don't blot their name out.' We burble about intercession. We chat to each other about burdens of prayer, but the man or the woman who has the real burden of prayer and the agony of the spirit of God upon his or her spirit in prayer loves and cares to the uttermost. Now I personally could not pray as Moses prayed, as Paul prayed (I try to be honest in spiritual things). I am not at a place where I could say, 'Lord, send me to hell if it would mean saving others.' Maybe I should be but I am not yet there. I can, however, stand with tremendous respect and observe a man like Moses and a man like Paul who so loved that they gave themselves to the uttermost and were prepared to go almost beyond the uttermost.

So Moses was not only the deliverer of Israel from Egypt under the mighty hand of God, but he was their saviour and preserver by an interceding power. He wrought gloriously, and no doubt it will one day be recognised before the throne of God. Yet, as we shall see shortly, he himself failed in a later crisis and never entered the land of promise. Because of the failure of an unhappy hour he was refused entry; it behoves men and women of God to walk carefully and obey God implicitly. In our early and inexperienced stages of spiritual life God seems to overlook a mountain of folly and restore our sinning souls. In mature years, when a person who actually knows God turns again to folly, the consequences can be disastrous. God would bring us into places of spiritual responsibility. He would have us become mature saints. He would have us learn to do what He tells us and not to do what our foolish minds dictate. Shall we come under His hand and His power? Shall we avoid the later mistake of Moses— which was at least partly the taking of the initiative by a man who should have known better?

In various of my earlier books I make reference to

intercession and I do not want to repeat this here. Let me say again, however, that I regard intercession as one of the most important ministries that is given to man. It is neither peripheral nor of secondary importance. It is vital and fundamental. Without it there can be weakness and defeat in the church. With real intercession (not merely general prayer) there comes glorious victory and fruitfulness. It should be amongst our first priorities. Study the lives of the great saints of God and observe the place they gave to it: Praying Hyde, Charles G. Finney, Father Nash, David Brainerd, Hudson Taylor, George Mueller, Rees Howells.* Do not neglect this area.

* Readers interested are referred to the author's *Reflections from Abraham* (New Dawn Books, 1989), chap. 4.

8

Rebellion in the Camp

It is fascinating to look back. People think it must have been wonderful to be a great man of God, to be like Moses, but does it ever occur to you how fearful it must have been to be in the positions Moses faced from time to time—not only in his dealings with Pharaoh in Egypt but through all his later days, when for example he went into the mountain of God and was terrified, or when he came down from Sinai and the people were worshipping the golden calf— the same people who had blamed Moses in their pain when his first interview with Pharaoh led to an increase of their burdens? Oh, it was no light thing being a leader of the people of God. At the Red Sea we have seen the reaction of the Israelites: Pharaoh's chariots murderously pursuing—no way back; the sea in front and no way through, and all the fault of Moses; but God—but God: *Stand still, and see the salvation of the LORD*: God opened a way where there was no way, and the people of God went through on dry land; the Egyptians, essaying to do so, were drowned in the midst of the sea as the waters returned, and Israel went over to the next stage of her journey. Deliverance from Egypt was complete.

As we study these things and meditate on them we become increasingly aware of the greatness of God. Not the greatness of Moses, but the mighty power of God over the devil and the power of the man of God over the devil's emissary in spite of the appearance of things, in spite of the seemingly likely outcome—the wonder of our God.

There are other incidents in the later life of Moses, not directly related to deliverance, that I would like to bring to your attention—again to help us to understand the ways of God with men and aspects of spiritual law that are little understood in our day. Three of these incidents in particular have come before me. Many people may be familiar with the parts of the story of Moses we have studied, but some may be less so with the rebellion of Aaron and Miriam and then of Korah, Dathan and Abiram against Moses and, secondly, with what was virtually the rebellion of Moses against God. The third incident—the giving of the law on Sinai—is very well known, but something of its inner significance for our own day is very largely undiscovered.

The first is a most strange incident:

And Miriam and Aaron spake against Moses because of the Cushite woman whom he had married: for he had married a Cushite woman. And they said, Hath the LORD indeed spoken only with Moses? hath he not spoken also with us? And the LORD heard it (Num 12:1–2).

The next verse is beautiful: *Now the man Moses was very meek, above all the men which were upon the face of the earth.* What a changed man from the early Moses!

And the LORD spake suddenly unto Moses, and unto Aaron, and unto Miriam, Come out ye three unto the tent of meeting. And they three came out. And the LORD came down in a pillar of cloud, and stood at the door of the Tent, and called Aaron and Miriam: and they both came forth. And he said, Hear now my words: if there be a prophet among you, I the LORD will make myself known unto him in a vision, I will speak with him in a dream. My servant Moses is not so: he is faithful in all mine house: With

*will I speak mouth to mouth, even manifestly, and not in dark
speeches; and the form of the* LORD *shall he behold: wherefore
then were ye not afraid to speak against my servant, against
Moses? And the anger of the* LORD *was kindled against them; and
he departed. And the cloud removed from over the Tent; and,
behold, Miriam was leprous, as white as snow: and Aaron looked
upon Miriam, and, behold, she was leprous. And Aaron said unto
Moses, Oh my lord, lay not, I pray thee, sin upon us, for that we
have done foolishly, and for that we have sinned. Let her not, I
pray, be as one dead, of whom the flesh is half consumed when he
cometh out of his mother's womb* (vv.4–12).

This is indeed a strange story. We are not told whether
Moses ought to have married the Cushite (Ethiopian)
woman or not, and if you read around the matter you may
understand something of what was in the mind of Aaron
and Miriam. A point, however, came when they said that
God had spoken to them as well as to Moses. It was as
though they failed to recognise the uniqueness of the
divine call that was on their brother and thought they too
were similarly called and had a right to their own opinions.
Basically they rebelled against Moses' leadership, and God
spoke suddenly in judgment. They failed to recognise the
degree of the anointing of God on His chosen leader, and
in opposing Moses they opposed God Himself.

I have always been impressed with the attitude of David
in a later day with regard to Saul. Saul sinned grievously
and God rejected him from being king over Israel. In his
jealousy he tried to kill David again and again, and David
could have retaliated and killed Saul, but he never did. He
refused to lift his hand against the Lord's anointed.

I am very thankful too that at an early stage in life I read
a book on the Scottish Covenanters in which one incident
in particular made a profound impression on me. One of
their leaders, Sandy Peden, was a very godly man. He was
a noted prophet[1], and one part of his story caught my
attention. A young preacher called Renwick had come
from the Continent and was very much in favour with the

Covenanters. He was a particularly able preacher and it may have been that a wisp of jealousy touched Sandy's spirit; in any case he spoke some words against him. Time passed, the months if not the years, until Sandy eventually met him and spoke words of great pathos and significance. He said that he so much wanted to meet Renwick because one day he had spoken a few words against him and from that day things had never been the same between God and himself. He wanted to meet the man whose relationship with God was such as to produce this effect.

Long since I have made a rule in relation to speaking about God's servants and I suggest that you should do the same. Occasionally I meet a preacher who may say or do things very differently from the way I would choose to do them, but for many years I have made a point of keeping my tongue off the Lord's anointed. You may sometimes wonder why God uses a particular person as He does. Leave that with God; He makes no mistakes. Did you ever wonder why God uses you—if He does! Always remember that while you are criticising a brother or sister, others may be criticising you.[2] You say, 'Does that mean that I should accept everything in the life of a person whom God uses?' Oh no, it does not, but *you* leave judgment with God and never exercise it unless it is in your legitimate sphere so to do.[3]

Immediately after Israel refused to go into Canaan, choosing to accept the report of the ten spies rather than that of Joshua and Caleb, the rebellion of Korah, Dathan and Abiram broke out.

Now Korah, the son of Izhar, the son of Kohath, the son of Levi, with Dathan and Abiram, the sons of Eliab, and On, the son of Peleth, sons of Reuben, took men: And they rose up before Moses, with certain of the children of Israel, two hundred and fifty princes of the congregation, called to the assembly, men of renown: And they assembled themselves together against Moses and against Aaron, and said unto them, Ye take too much upon you, seeing all the congregation are holy, every one of them, and the LORD is

among them: wherefore then lift ye up yourselves above the assem-
bly of the LORD? And when Moses heard it, he fell upon his face
(Num 16:1–4).

The judgment which resulted was fearful, first with the
destruction of the principal rebels and their immediate
followers and then of 14,700 others.

If these men die the common death of all men, or if they be visited
after the visitation of all men, then the LORD hath not sent me.
But if the LORD make a new thing, and the ground open her
mouth, and swallow them up, with all that appertain unto them,
and they go down alive into the pit; then ye shall understand that
these men have despised the LORD. And it came to pass, as he
made an end of speaking all these words, that the ground clave
asunder that was under them: And the earth opened her mouth,
and swallowed them up, and their households, and all the men
that appertained unto Korah, and all their goods (Num 16: 29–
33).

Immediately after this rebellion, we read:

But on the morrow all the congregation of the children of Israel
murmured against Moses and against Aaron, saying, Ye have
killed the people of the LORD (v.41).

Instead of a sense of awe at the divine judgment on a
grossly rebellious company, it seems that a wave of sympathy went out to them and the people murmured against
Moses and Aaron, accusing them of killing the people of
God. They did not kill the people of God. The rebellious
renegades in effect committed suicide. They brought on
their own heads the just judgment of God. They were
guilty of rebellion, and rebellion, God tells us plainly, is
'as the sin of witchcraft' and punishable by death.

Throughout the ages and in our own day human reac-
tions tend to remain the same. We judge rebellion lightly.
God judges it severely. We sympathise with those on
whom judgment falls. God expects a firm reaction from us

and a refusal to condone any degree of rebellion. Let leaders exercise firm discipline on a church member, leading perhaps to excommunication, and observe the consequences. Many will judge the leaders as harsh, and a wave of sympathy is very likely to go out to the defaulter. The leaders are apt to be murmured against and a spirit of rebellion engendered. Basically we tend to have too little of the fear of the living God in our hearts and too light a conception of the seriousness of entertaining any rebellious thought against either Him or His anointed and appointed servants.

Notes

1   There are lovely stories about Sandy Peden. When the dragoons were trying to catch him on one occasion and almost did, he said that the Lord just put down a corner of His mantle and covered old Sandy. The mist came down and hid him: Sandy was in God's cloak and Sandy was safe. From time to time he gave very accurate predictions. One very interesting one related to a place in Greenock, my own home town. An old building which stood very close to IBM's modern site had become a ruin through the years. In so far as I can remember the prophecy, Sandy had been refused admittance at a critical juncture, and he predicted that the building would become derelict and that *the highways of the world* would pass through it. Now it was that last expression that was particularly interesting. What did Sandy mean, 'the highways of the world'? The place is not far from the Clyde and the words did not seem terribly relevant. Through the centuries the building stood. Eventually IBM came along and built beside it but left it standing. Many watched to see if Sandy's prediction would be fulfilled, but there it still stood. The day came, however, when it was decided to have a new road built, and down the ruins came—but what of Sandy's 'highways of the world'? Think of IBM with all its international connections; this new road was to convey goods not only within Britain but to the world. It went right through the place where the ruin stood: the old building was obliterated as Sandy had predicted. For

years people had waited to see if such a thing would ever happen—and how wonderful was the fulfilment!

2 I was much impressed with an illustration which I once heard from a Rhuanda missionary. Pointing his index finger at someone, he said, 'Notice that when I point *one* finger at you, *three* are pointing back at me.' Were it not so serious it could be amusing to hear Christians deplore the condition of their fellows. They wonder how some poor soul could have been so sinful! There, I usually feel, go hypocrites. A normal person knows very well how easy it is to commit normal sin. (I do not speak of deep abnormality, which sometimes may only be understood in terms of demon possession. Evil produces deepening evil and evildoers graduate to deepening levels of wickedness in stages—as saints progress to higher levels of holiness stage by stage.) Often the critic is in much worse case than the person criticised. Perhaps the following poem, entitled 'Fancy Meeting You,' will make the point effectively.

> I dreamt death came the other night
>   And Heaven's gate swung wide;
> An angel with a halo bright
>   Ushered me inside.
>
> And there to my astonishment
>   Were folks I'd judged and labelled
> As 'quite unfit,' 'of little worth,'
>   And 'spiritually disabled.'
>
> Indignant words rose to my lips
>   But never were set free:
> For every face showed stunned surprise—
>   No one expected me!

3 As it could be, for example, if you are in a position of authority such as that of pastor or elder when discipline involving the judgment of individuals may be necessary.

9

The Failure of Moses

The next incident is also fearful. There was a serious shortage of water, and the people murmured bitterly against Moses. God instructed His servant to speak to the Rock. Now previously water had come out of the Rock when he had struck it at God's command. This time the command was not to strike but to speak. This was a rare occasion when we see a flash of anger in Moses. Both he and Aaron seemed to claim something which was not theirs. They said: *Shall we bring you forth water out of this rock?* (Num 20:10) Moses then struck the Rock. We read in the New Testament that the Rock that followed them was Christ. There was symbolism in this. Christ would once be smitten on the cross and would never be smitten again. Men would never after the cross get anything from Christ by smiting, although they would drink of the water of life as a result of the first smiting. Thereafter they would speak to the Rock. Moses sinned, and the consequences were dire:

> *And the LORD said unto Moses and Aaron, Because ye believed not in me, to sanctify me in the eyes of the chldren of Israel, therefore ye shall not bring this assembly into the land which I have given them. These are the waters of Meribah; because the*

children of Israel strove with the LORD, and he was sanctified in them (Num 20:12–13).

Later we hear Moses say:

> *And I besought the LORD at that time, saying, O LORD God, thou hast begun to shew thy servant thy greatness, and thy strong hand: for what god is there in heaven or in earth, that can do according to thy works, and according to thy mighty acts? Let me go over, I pray thee, and see the good land that is beyond Jordan, that goodly mountain, and Lebanon. But the LORD was wroth with me for your sakes, and hearkened not unto me: and the LORD said unto me, Let it suffice thee; speak no more unto me of this matter. Get thee up into the top of Pisgah, and lift up thine eyes westward, and northward, and southward, and eastward, and behold with thine eyes: for thou shalt not go over this Jordan. But charge Joshua, and encourage him, and strengthen him: for he shall go over before this people, and he shall cause them to inherit the land which thou shalt see* (Deut 3:23–28).

Lord, this is Your mighty servant Moses. And, Lord, he has done so much for You.—No, he has not: I have done so much through him.—Lord, he has been begging You in prayer to let him go into the land.—Yes, and I will hear him no more on this matter! A dictate has gone out: a judgment has been made, and it will not be changed.

> *And Moses went up from the plains of Moab unto mount Nebo, to the top of Pisgah, that is over against Jericho. And the LORD shewed him all the land of Gilead, unto Dan; And all Naphtali, and the land of Ephraim and Manasseh, and all the land of Judah, unto the hinder sea; And the South, and the Plain of the valley of Jericho the city of palm trees, unto Zoar. And the LORD said unto him, This is the land which I sware unto Abraham, unto Isaac, and unto Jacob, saying, I will give it unto thy seed: I have caused thee to see it with thine eyes, but thou shalt not go over thither. So Moses the servant of the LORD died there in the land of Moab, according to the word of the LORD. . . . And there hath not arisen a prophet since in Israel like unto Moses, whom the LORD knew face to face; In all the signs and the wonders, which the*

LORD *sent him to do in the land of Egypt, to Pharaoh, and to all his servants, and to all his land; And in all the mighty hand, and in all the great terror, which Moses wrought in the sight of all Israel* (Deut 34:1–5, 10–12).

From these events I have learned one thing. God is God. God is holy. You don't touch God. You never put out your hand to steady the ark of God. You die the death if you do. God is God. I indicated earlier that I wanted you to comprehend something of the greatness of God. People who are very deeply used of God have one thing in common—they have a consciousness of God's greatness, of His holiness. They are in awe of the touch of the divine: they know the fear of the Lord.

Where these matters were concerned Pharaoh was as a beast and he died the death of a beast. Korah and his company were ungodly rebels and they died a dreadful death. Aaron and Miriam probably did not fully understand the seriousness of their actions and there was forgiveness, but for Moses the mature servant of God it was very dangerous to err as he did. It is always dangerous to sin from a position of maturity: sins which are easily forgiven in early days may not be indulged in with impunity at deeper levels of spiritual life. God's standards are very high and He holds us fully responsible when He has given deep knowledge. Moses, I believe, was still regarded by God as one of the greatest of all men who had ever lived or ever would live, but even upon such a man, at the moment he infringed the divine law, dreadful consequences fell. There was and is no respect of persons with God, and Moses could not act as he did with impunity. We must never move against the Holy One. You may sin many kinds of sins, but never sin that sin: none who ever does escapes.

10

The God of Sinai

*And be ready against the third day: for the third day the LORD
will come down in the sight of all the people upon mount Sinai.
And thou shalt set bounds unto the people round about, saying,
Take heed to yourselves, that ye go not up into the mount, or touch
the border of it: whosoever toucheth the mount shall be surely put
to death.... And it came to pass on the third day, when it
was morning, that there were thunders and lightnings, and a
thick cloud upon the mount, and the voice of a trumpet exceeding
loud; and all the people that were in the camp trembled (Ex 19:11–
12, 16).*

God's hour had come for the giving of the law and of the
revelation of more of Himself to His people. It was an
awesome hour and one which should never be forgotten.
We live in an age when there is frequently a very light
attitude to God and to holy things even amongst reputedly
good Christian people. There is an approach to God which
is overfamiliar and totally mistaken. On that occasion the
people were required to prepare themselves days before
the coming of God and to be most circumspect in their
approach. Even so they were in fear and ultimately asked
Moses to go before God on their behalf. In the epistle to
the Hebrews the matter is put into proper perspective and

the attitude of Moses and the effect of his meeting with
God noted:

> *For ye are not come unto a mount that might be touched, and that
> burned with fire, and unto blackness, and darkness, and tempest,
> And the sound of a trumpet, and the voice of words; which voice
> they that heard intreated that no word more should be spoken unto
> them: For they could not endure that which was enjoined, If even
> a beast touch the mountain, it shall be stoned; And so fearful was
> the appearance, that Moses said, I exceedingly fear and quake*
> (Heb 12:18–21).

As I comment in an earlier book,

> When God came down on Sinai men fled from the base of the
> mountain. *If even a beast touch the mountain, it shall be stoned*,
> and so fearful was the appearance that Moses said, *I exceed-*
> *ingly fear and quake*. That mighty man of God was profoundly
> affected at the drawing near of God. Ponder this. By this time
> in his life Moses was already a seasoned vessel. He had been
> deeply used of God. He had been present when the bush
> burned with fire. At God's command he had appeared before
> the face of Pharaoh, working mighty signs and witnessing
> mighty miracles. He had led Israel over the Red Sea through
> divine intervention. He was no novice. Yet at Sinai this man
> was exceedingly afraid.*

We do well to ponder this. Remember too the place of
godly fear in Scripture. Jacob swore by the fear of his
father Isaac. When he saw the ladder going up to Heaven
at Bethel and the angels of God going up and down on it,
he said, *How dreadful is this place! this is none other than the*
house of God, and this is the gate of heaven (Gen 28:17). In a
later day the apostle John, the disciple peculiarly loved by
Christ, did not greet his Lord with familiarity when he

---

*Reflections on the Baptism in the Holy Spirit (New Dawn Books, 1987),
pp.38–9.

met Him on ascension ground on Patmos isle. He fell at His feet as one dead.

When times of revival come to the church, there comes a peculiar awe, a God-consciousness. Light, frothy attitudes change in a moment of time. God is as a consuming fire. When that day comes, when we stand before God we will not behave in a jaunty, irreverent way, but with deep seriousness and reverence.

This same God was to come down on the day of Pentecost as recorded in Acts 2:

> And when the day of Pentecost was now come, they were all together in one place. And suddenly there came from heaven a sound as of the rushing of a mighty wind, and it filled all the house where they were sitting. And there appeared unto them tongues parting asunder, like as of fire; and it sat upon each one of them. And they were all filled with the Holy Spirit, and began to speak with other tongues, as the Spirit gave them utterance (Acts 2:1–4).

If I may again quote from my earlier work:*

Christians are generally aware that Pentecost came fifty days after passover—but it is not so widely known that Pentecost fell on the anniversary of the coming of God on Sinai. A few scholars have noticed this, but the significance of the fact seems to have been almost completely overlooked.

There is an almost jubilant note in the description of the coming of the Spirit on the day of Pentecost and surely those who tarried were in need of a jubilant note. They had been very deeply prepared. After the awful hours of Calvary, their own general defection, the dark days when He lay in the tomb, the surprised joy of resurrection, they were in no danger of taking the things of God lightly. Theirs had been a traumatic experience.

I have noticed in our day that Christians frequently seek

---

*The remainder of this chapter is taken with slight modification from *Reflections on the Baptism*, pp. 37–41.

the baptism in the Spirit much too lightly. They seem to forget that an encounter with God is involved. They have not known the trauma which the early Christians experienced and often come unprepared. In addition, salvation has frequently also been lightly presented and a knowledge of the holiness and majesty of God is too often lacking. In these circumstances, I have found in moving under the leading of God, the first sound that falls on their ears is not the jubilant note of Pentecost but the thunder of Sinai.

...We have an almost immediate reaction as we read the account in Hebrews. We are glad that ours is the dispensation of grace and not of law. We sense the awfulness of the former and are relieved. One can almost hear the sigh of relief as the church goes on to read:

For ye are not come unto a mount that might be touched, and that burned with fire, and unto blackness... (Heb 12:18).

How thankful we are to be in the dispensation of grace. With what pleasant sound come the words:

But ye are come unto mount Zion, and unto the city of the living God, the heavenly Jerusalem, and to innumerable hosts of angels, to the general assembly and church of the firstborn who are enrolled in heaven, and to God the Judge of all, and to the spirits of just men made perfect, and to Jesus the mediator of a new covenant, and to the blood of sprinkling that speaketh better than that of Abel (Heb 12:22–24).

Yes. This is the position we know. We love the idea of drawing near to Zion and to the heavenly Jerusalem. It seems so lovely and comfortable and in keeping with our conception of a God of love. We may have only vague ideas about *innumerable hosts of angels* and *the spirits of just men made perfect* and pass quickly over the reference to *God the Judge of all*; but surely we can rejoice in the idea of drawing near to *Jesus the mediator of a new covenant* and to *the blood of sprinkling that speaketh better than that of Abel*.

But then comes the shock. We go on to read:

See that ye refuse not him that speaketh. For if they escaped not, when they refused him that warned them on earth, much more shall not we escape, who turn away from him that warneth from heaven: whose voice then shook the earth: but now hath promised, saying, Yet once more will I make to tremble not the earth only, but also the heaven. And this word, Yet once more, signifieth the removing of those things that are shaken, as of things that have been made, that those things which are not shaken may remain (Heb 12:25–27).

Suddenly there comes the dawning awareness that the interpretation may be wholly mistaken. It was a dreadful thing to refuse the voice which warned from earth. The voice now warns from Heaven: *Much more shall not we escape, who turn away.* In that day the voice shook the earth but now there is a promise to make tremble not only earth but Heaven. In short, it was a fearful thing to disobey the voice that spoke from Sinai in the old dispensation; it is a more fearful and dangerous thing to disobey the voice that now speaks from Heaven. Disobedient man is not now in a more comfortable but in a much less comfortable position. And in addition 'things shaken' will now be removed. There will be judgment and destruction for refusing to obey the voice that speaks in the dispensation of grace. Gradually we begin to realise something of the character of God. And finally we read: *Wherefore, receiving a kingdom that cannot be shaken, let us have grace, whereby we may offer service well-pleasing to God with reverence and awe: for our God is a consuming fire.* We should always remember that while God is a God of pardoning grace and love, He is still the God of Sinai. Do not let us imagine that there is any change in His character or demands as we pass from the dispensation of law to the dispensation of grace. Our obligations become more rather than less exacting. Note carefully that our service should be *with reverence and awe*: there should be no light, frothy, casual, familiar approach to God. *Our God is a consuming fire.* Let us ponder these words and ponder them deeply. This is the God with Whom we have to do. Let us always remember this as we approach Him.

This God came down on Sinai and men could not abide His coming. The same God is to come down at Pentecost and this time men do not flee in fear—but God comes right down and enters their very bodies. What has happened? What has made it possible? The cross has happened! They are clean by His blood and able to be filled with the Holy One. What kind of experience is this? Surely holy, awesome, glorious, terrible, and so with reverence and awe let us approach our Pentecost!

PART 2

THE TESTIMONY
OF
DAN McVICAR

Author's Introduction

Before I ever met Danny McVicar I had heard much about him, and from earlier years I carry two particular memories. On one occasion, maybe twenty years ago, Danny and Mr John Anderson were present at a Scottish Pentecostal leaders' meeting, and the issue of what was then known as 'revelation' ministry was being hotly debated. John was an early pioneer in 'deliverance' ministry and Danny was, I believe, receiving clear words of knowledge in his ministry. There was a good deal of opposition to the idea of special revelation in these early days and I had the privilege of standing with these two brethren on that occasion. Neither was a theologian, but they did produce results. I was never in any doubt of the scriptural basis of their activity, and it was a joy to be identified with them then.

As the years have passed and increasing numbers of eminent men of God have been used in powerful 'revelation' ways, controversy within Pentecostal circles has tended to die. The evidence is just too strong.

My second vivid memory is of a night in Harthill. I had been invited to preach at the closing meeting of a convention in the Pentecostal church in that village. I arrived there on my way home to Greenock from a series of meetings in Bradford. Memory is a strange thing. I remember in sharp detail various matters related to that

occasion, whereas nowadays I can forget important events
of a week ago. I remember the Bradford meetings. I
remember a heavily made-up lady receiving her baptism in
the Spirit and the tears making rivulets down her cheeks
through, I presume, mascara and rouge. I was rejoicing
and vocalised my joy, when I suddenly felt I was rejoicing
alone. The silence around was ominous. (The church was
not as Pentecostal as I expected such churches to be, and
its teaching on the baptism in the Spirit was different from
mine.) I next went to an older man, who said, 'I've been
seeking for sixteen years, but I've never spoken in
tongues.' I said, 'Well, brother, you'll be speaking in
tongues within about two minutes.' Some might say,
'Faith,' others, 'Presumption.' Some might see an element
of revelation. In any case the man was filled and spoke
fluently as predicted.

I came north to Harthill and oddly enough I remember
the sermon to this day. I seemed to have a very clear
revelation of the infinite power of God like an ocean above
us, with an area of almost infinite need around us. The
power was to come down through human channels. The
relevant texts were: *All authority hath been given unto me*
(Mat 28:18), *Ye shall receive power, when the Holy Ghost is
come upon you* (Acts 1:8), and *The gospel...is the power of
God unto salvation* (Rom 1:16).

Immediately after the sermon I called for a 'tarry' meeting[1] and we met in a kind of small side-chapel. Danny was
there, and Danny was in his element in a tarry meeting. I
don't now remember how many were seeking, or how
many received, but I do remember one old lady who was
seeking. She turned to me and said, and I could hardly
believe my ears, 'I've been seeking for sixteen years and
while I get anointings I have never spoken in tongues.'
Again I heard myself say something like, 'Don't worry,
you'll be speaking in tongues in about two minutes,' and,
praise God, she was. I found the coincidence of these two
people waiting so long and both receiving so quickly

remarkable. Soon afterwards Danny, like the old Method-
ists—Billy Bray, for example—began to get happy. He
got a hold of two chairs, turned them back to back in the
aisle and swung on them. Up went his legs and down went
Danny amongst the wreckage! I, for my part, was taking a
serious meeting and was no doubt expected to maintain a
solemn countenance in the midst of these proceedings.
Danny was and still is, as his testimony shows, full of fun.

The following testimony is taken largely from a tape
recording made a few years ago when he preached in
Struthers Memorial Church. For the sake of English ears
some of the 'Doric' has been translated. Sometimes it has
been retained. It is his native language, and to replace it
could spoil the effect. At times in his testimony interesting
sidelines arose and he digressed. I have tended to follow
the digressions and while this may not seem to conform to
traditional ways of presenting a testimony, it may make for
more interesting reading.

Danny has deliberately soft-pedalled the darker parts of
his early sinful days, but I can assure you that things were
much worse than the picture he presents. He really was a
bondservant of Satan and deeply and violently in his service. Not only was he a slave to alcohol but he was a
militant communist and his militancy was not merely the-
oretical. We will leave the veil which he does not wish to
lift. I should perhaps mention that at the time of giving
this testimony Danny was eighty-two years of age.

Note

[1] 'Tarry' is a term more frequently used then than now. It
derived from the command of Christ: *Tarry ye in the city, until
ye be clothed with power from on high* (Lk 24:49). We used the
term 'tarry meeting' to describe a meeting specifically con-
vened for the receiving of the baptism in the Spirit.

The Testimony of Dan McVicar

Therefore if any man be in Christ, he is a new creature: old things are passed away; behold, all things are become new (2 Cor 5:17 AV).

I want tonight to prove to you the truth of this word. It is my testimony.

My wife and I have just come back from Worcester where we saw God save many souls. We had to stay for seven weeks as blessing fell. It was a marvellous time. One lady who had worn calipers for years took them off after prayer; God miraculously healed her and she walked home with her calipers under her arm.

Another young lady of about twenty-five had a tumour behind her left eye, and this had begun to break out on her cheek. She sat hidden at the back of the church, not wanting anybody to see her condition. The pus was running down her cheek. She had been given a scan and it was discovered that the tumour was deep and growing fast. The word of knowledge came to me and I said, 'There's a woman here, and you've been at hospital and had bad news: you've a tumour behind the left eye, and it's broken out on your cheek.' The girl came out immediately and was prayed for. If there had been any sceptics there they could have had a lot to say, because it seemed as though nothing happened. I believed that God had touched her.

We left the area and then we had a postcard from Cornwall, where the family had gone on holiday. They wrote: 'We'll tell you all about what happened when we come home. The girl is with us. Two days after she was prayed for the cheek healed up. She went to the hospital, where they gave her another scan and couldn't find any tumour.' God had healed it! That's the Christ that I serve. Maybe you're amazed at me shouting, 'Praise the Lord!' When you hear my testimony, you'll realise the reason.

I was an atheist, an agnostic—never was in a church or a Sunday school in my life. I'm still friendly with an agnostic—believes in nothing. Every time I meet him, he wants to take a bit o' a chitter out o' me. The last time we met, he said to me, 'Dae ye still go to these meetins'?'

I said, 'I do. And I expect to go there till the trumpet sounds.'

'Well, I'm amazed,' he said, 'at the age you are, and believin' in these fairy-tales.'

I said, 'Tell me one. I'm not askin' for half-a-dozen; just tell me one.'

And wi' a chitter about him he said, 'Well, what about Jonah?'

I said, 'Just a minute. You've just mentioned one o' my favourite characters. That's the fella who went away in a ship and came back in a submarine.' And I said, 'Before you tell me anything about Jonah, let me tell you something.' (You've got to get in first with an atheist, you know.) 'Let me tell you something. When I get up there, I'm goin' to have a long talk wi' Jonah on all his escapades.'

He said, 'Oh, aye. But what if he's no' up there?'

I said, 'Well, then, you can talk tae him.'

And that finished the conversation. He said, 'Ye're well away, ye're well away—I cannae talk tae ye.'

I want to give you my testimony tonight. Let me say honestly, friends: I would rather minister—because in giving personal testimony there seems to be so much

'I...I...me.' But tonight I want to glorify God and I don't want to wash any dirty linen in public. I visit many churches, and hear many testimonies, and I'm often horrified. People tell of the horrible things they've done and the horrible places they've lived, and the devil gets more glory than God. Well, I want to tell you tonight how God changed my life and I want to glorify Him. You will be able to read between the lines, as I give my testimony, of where I've been, of how I've lived and of the things I've done. And I want to begin from the very beginning.

I was born and brought up in an unsaved family: thirteen of us. First up was best dressed. It was a survival o' the fittest. Well, I'm one that survived. I longed for the day when I would leave school. I absolutely hated school. I plugged it (played truant) more often than I attended it. You know, in those days there were no O-levels: it wasn't O-levels, it was No-levels, and I had every one of them. The rest of my family used to come home with their reports on grammar and history and whatnot, and I used to burn mine. I remember Dad saying, 'Where is yours?' and I said, 'The teacher kep' it.' 'Kep' it what fur?' 'Just as an example,' I said, 'to show the rest.' 'To show the rest?' he said. 'Aye—how much I've learned and so little bein' there. It's a marvel tae her.'

I longed for the day when I would leave school and become a man. And I did leave one Friday night at the age of thirteen, and that night the teachers had a party. I didn't have an invitation. It was because of me going they were rejoicing. Yes, I left school on the Friday night at the age of thirteen, and I was down the mine on the Monday morning—only a lad. In those days it was downright slavery, from early morning till late at night, and very little being paid for it. That put something in my spirit and in my heart, a sourness against capitalism. I hated it, I hated the very word, with all that was within me. I determined that when I became of age or even before I became of age if there were anything I could do to hinder the progression of capitalism I would do it. As a young lad I joined the YCP, the Young Communist Party. The night that God saved me I was an ardent worker for communism. I was a disciple of Trotsky and Lenin, and sat at the feet of the late Harry Pollitt—he was my teacher from Bellshill. In those days I believed the only remedy for this world was what happened in Russia—a bloodthirsty revolution: oh yes, I believed it. I became bloodthirsty to change the system of the world, and I became an ardent worker for communism.

My work brought me into the hands of the police. I had been in the hands of the police before that. I've stood in the juvenile court, I've stood in the sheriff court, and I've stood in the High Court (and I'm ashamed to tell you these things). I want to tell you tonight: crime does not pay, and neither does the law thrash sin out of any man. Nothing can change man but Jesus Christ, and I thank God for it. I had a hope, I lived in hope that one day I'd become an MP for North Lanark. That was my ambition in life. My dad was a wrestler: he took the Scottish championship from Alf Stone the showman. And I had a brother, Billy, who was a professional boxer. But I was absolutely nothing. I was the black sheep of the family. Never was in a Sunday school, never was in a church in my life. I began to drink at the age of fifteen, and began to gamble. I loved the pleasure of the world. I'm not here to tell you there is no pleasure in the world—there is. There's great pleasure in the world. But God's Word declares clearly, it's the pleasure of sin for a season. The joy I've got will never end. On Saturday nights I used to have champagne and on Sunday morning I had real pain. There was nothing sham about it. I lived a reckless life, friends, as a young man. And let me tell you honestly: I believe, if it hadn't been for the grace of God, I'd have been an alcoholic tonight, if I'd been alive at all. Or I might have been doing a stretch in Barlinnie or Saughton—as it is, I'm in there often enough, preaching the gospel. Indeed, there were eight souls saved last

Thursday night in Shotts Prison, and we're going in again this Thursday night. We're seeing prisoners saved, in prison. They're not all bad in prison, you know. It's only because some of them are chicken, getting involved because of their pals. Did you ever hear the story of the old minister who visited the prison to the horror of an old woman in his church—horror that her minister was going into prison to visit these persons? And she said, 'Parson, what kind of people did you find in there?' 'The same as you and me, madam,' he said, 'but they were found out.' That was the only difference!

So I enjoyed the pleasures of the world. I enjoyed the dance hall, I enjoyed the gambling den with the tossing of the pennies, and I enjoyed the card school—all of it. I didn't back many winners among the horses, friends... it was donkeys I backed, donkeys. I always say the ruination of man is fast women and slow horses. I lived a life, friends—and it would be a shame to tell you of the places I lived in as a teenager. Sometimes I would win, and four of us who ran together and slept together (we were never separate) used to go away on Friday nights after winning. And, friends, my old, ungodly mother never saw me till a Tuesday or a Wednesday—and I would come back home with not a tosser. There I was—I walked from Edinburgh sometimes back to Harthill, or from Glasgow straight to Canongate, and slept under benches at night, and there we lived. We thought we were having a real kick in life. That's how I lived. I loved the pleasures of the world—I was steeped in them. An ardent worker in communism, an atheist, an agnostic, I believed in absolutely nothing— except that as a tree falls, so shall it lie. That was the end of everything—I believed in annihilation. No hereafter, nothing else. But God was in things all the time. Friends, there's one thing that thrills me in my salvation. I was thrilled when I read in God's Word that even when I was in my mother's womb His hand had been upon me. Glory to God! That thrills me. In all my wayward life, in everything I did, God's hand had been upon me. And I thank God that He spared me to the night I got saved.

When I was at home, I used to come up the street drunk on a Saturday night—I lived on the laurels of my dad and my brother the boxer. I used to shout on the street, filled with Dutch courage: 'I've never refused a challenge in my life. I'll take on anything in this street—and come out in your two's if you like.' Likely if two had come I would have fainted! There I boasted, Saturday night after Saturday night. But I wasn't exempt from hearing the gospel. A young woman used to meet me on the street on a Saturday night when I was at home. She was out fishing—giving out tracts on the street. She used to meet me, and there she would preach the gospel to me. I would laugh at her—I would make a fool of her, and as she gave me tracts I used to tear them up in pieces, like confetti, and scatter them all over her hair, and try to joke with her and make a fool of her. But I tell you this, friends, I never could ruffle her. While I ruffled her hair, I never could ruffle her. She was a hell-fire preacher. And if there's anything I love today it's hell-fire preachers: they're scarce today. She used to hang me over hell for a few minutes, and when she left me I felt like a smoked kipper! I certainly did. And all the time she was working on me, her idea was to get me saved. But I never believed in God—I didn't want to believe in God. And don't let me get your back up when I tell you this. While I've thrown off communism—I live for Christ—I still believe the saying of Karl Marx that religion is the dope of the masses. And that's true. The devil can blind you sitting in a fashionable church, feeling safe and all right, and feeling lovely in the church, all the time being blindfolded with religion, never knowing that while you're there and feeling comfortable you're on your way to an undone eternity. Religion is the dope of the masses. I haven't got religion, I've got Jesus Christ—and that's the vital thing. It was He Who changed my life. *If any man be in Christ, he is a new creature*. I tell you tonight, I'm a new creation, I'm a brand new man. God changed me completely.

This is how it happened. I was sitting at a gambling school one Sunday afternoon, late afternoon, playing at pontoon. There were four schools, one of our group in each school: we never played against one another. All of a sudden there was an invasion, as a band of young people, young men and women from Harthill Pentecostal Church, descended upon us and began to give out tracts. You might have thought they would be afraid. I was well known in the village. I was in every court. I was known in many districts as I used to stand on the ginger box at street corners and preach communism. But no matter, there they were—an invasion. And the young woman who used to preach to me in the street walked right round the school. I (who never had a collar and tie on in my life) was sitting there in a black muffler, small jacket and bell-mouthed trousers: that was the style. She tapped me on the shoulder and said,

'I've a message for you from God.'

And I said to her, 'Buzz off—buzz off!'

I tell you, friends, she met me in an evil hour. I was losing at the time, and I wasn't in a very good mood. I said to her, 'There's no such person—there's no such person as God Almighty. There's none at all—it's fables. Buzz off, and don't annoy me, and I'll tell you more—don't ever stop me on the street again and preach to me.'

She said, 'I don't care what you say. I'm delivering the message.'

I said, 'If you don't move, girl and all as you are, I'll flatten you on that grass.'

She said, 'I'll still can talk.' Oh, you trust a woman—phew! She said, 'I'm delivering the message before I go, whether you listen or not. I'm delivering it. I hear you shouting on the street on a Saturday night, you've "never refused a challenge". I've come to challenge you.'

Boy, I felt my hair stand up. I said to her, 'Buzz off.'

She said, 'I've come to challenge you. I hear you shouting on the street on a Saturday night that you've never refused a challenge. All right,' she said, 'You may not be afraid of anything in the village, but you're downright afraid to come to a gospel meeting. There's the message. Do what you like with it.'

Oh, I was fizzing. And when I looked, there were more spots than there should have been on the cards. It was spots before my eyes, with sheer anger! I was angry—and she only took half a dozen steps and looked back at me, and she said, 'If I don't see your face in the church, I'll take it that you're a coward.' Nobody ever told me I was a coward: nobody. And I tell you, the message got home.

She wasn't finished with me. She took another half step, and then she said, 'I'm finished with this one. You're not only a coward if you don't come... *you're yellow.*'

Oh, boy. What a mood I was in! I was trembling all over with sheer anger. And one of the boys said to me, 'Calm down.'

I said, 'I wish it had been some of the boys who had talked to me. I would have killed them.'

Friends, if she had told me of the love of God, I never would have got the message. God knows the bait to use when He goes fishing, especially when He goes fishing for sharks! I was a land shark, in more ways than one: a land shark! I'm cutting out the filthy things about it, friends, but I lived a life of shame and debauchery, and gambling and burgling and stealing and whatnot. (Do I see that policeman in the audience with his book out?) That's the type of life I lived, friends. And here was a woman challenging me, and telling me that I was yellow, I was a coward, if she didn't see my face in the meeting.

I flung down the cards, and I said to the boys, 'I'm taking that challenge up.'

A group leader in the communist party—and I was determined to go there and then to the meeting. I knew when the meeting came out. I knew when every church came out: I used to stand at the door with communist pamphlets and argue with them about their belief in this benevolent old gentleman in the skies they called God, and the mess He was making of the world. 'There's nobody up there at all,' I would say. Oh, yes, I knew when the meeting came out. And so I made up my mind: ten minutes before it came out, I would go in. I didn't know whether they prayed or what they did, but I would only have ten minutes to suffer whatever they did. And I slipped in the door to an empty seat at the back, and I sat there. I looked at my watch before I went in. The next time I looked at it, a quarter of an hour had passed—a quarter of an hour! Long-winded preacher! And let me tell you, you laymen who are here, and you women preachers who are here: if you don't strike oil in ten minutes, stop boring. You know the story of the long-winded preacher?—The minister was going on and on and on, and no sign of him stopping at all; a young man in the middle of the church, absolutely fed up, bored stiff, rose to go out, and the minister stopped and said to him, 'Hey, where are you going?' The young man looked round at him and said, 'I'm going home to shave.' 'Shave?' he said, 'you should have shaved before you came!' He said, 'I did!' That certainly was a long-winded preacher! And I felt the same about that fellow: long-winded. I rose there and then and went out and banged the door, and looked back to see if it was still on its hinges. I banged the door so that that young girl sitting there would realise I had been in: I had accepted the challenge.

Can I tell you something? The damage was done. When I went home, I discovered something was wrong with me, and I couldn't diagnose it. I can tell you now, I was under conviction. No psychiatrist can ever diagnose conviction, friends. It's only God: it's from God. For a whole week, when I came home from my work I sat down, then I walked up and down, and I smoked cigarette after cigarette. For a whole week!

On the following Saturday night my dad said to me, 'Boy, you've got me up the wall. You've got me dizzy watching you. You've got a pad made on that carpet back and forward. Look,' he said, 'I want to tell you something. You know where the boys are. Well, get out beside them. And if you don't, I'm sending for a doctor. You're on the verge of a breakdown—it's a mental asylum for you.'

A lot of folk think I should be in it now! I tell you, I'm sane enough—thank God for that. I see souls saved every week, I see bodies healed, I see people baptised in the Spirit. I believe, friends, we're on the verge of a move. I believe that. We're living in the last of the last days, when God's going to pour His Spirit out.

There I was under conviction, and I never went out: never went out. You talk about the love of God? Well, I didn't think He had any love. I didn't think there was any love in it. Sunday came, and half an hour before the church meeting a group from Harthill Pentecostal Church held an open-air outside our door, and there was myself under conviction marching up and down. And you talk about the love of God? He was pouring salt on my wounds! It certainly wasn't the cure for me—that's what I thought. When I lifted the curtain and looked out, there was this big fellow with a small concertina, and he was laughing from ear to ear and singing. And I said, 'Well, there's only one way to stop that. I'll go out and I'll kick that machine up in the air, and if he says anything he goes up along with it!' And I sure would have done it. I certainly would. I never remember the time when I was afraid of anything or any man.

I went to open the door and I couldn't raise the latch, friends. God was in it. I came back and sat down—and my dad's sitting watching me out of the corner of his eye: sitting watching me.

Then they began to sing a hymn. And if there's any

hymn that I love in my campaigns, it's 'Have you been to Jesus for the cleansing power?' It doesn't ask you if you have been to church, it doesn't ask you if you have been to mass; it asks, 'Have you been to Jesus?' That's the source of all life—that's the root of all life: Jesus Christ. 'Nothing can for sin atone, nothing but the blood of Jesus.' There and then a desire entered my heart to go back to that Pentecostal church. And the devil—I'll tell you, he's much alive; if you don't believe in a devil, I do. He's followed me—he's followed me—in fact, the last four months in different meetings the devil has manifested himself.

We went to a meeting, friends, in Market Harborough, and all of a sudden when I was preaching there was a darkness, and I couldn't preach—*I couldn't preach*. I said, 'Friends, there's something wrong here. The atmosphere's polluted. Somebody here has brought the devil in, or the devil has brought you in, just to split up this meeting. He's not going to do it.' And all of a sudden I said, 'It's you. You belong to a spiritualist church. You're playing around with the ouija board. In three days' time you've to go and meet a company of people and you've to sign your name in your own blood to become a satanist.'* And he just rose and stamped his two feet and began to dance, and the froth came out of his mouth. An elder rose to put his hand on him to tell him to simmer down, and he just lifted the elder like a child, and banged him against a chair, against the wall. God said to me, 'Get into action. I'm with you.' And I caught him by the wrist, and I held him, and I said, 'You're a filthy creature. You're coming out.' A scream went round the whole church, and the demon said, 'I'm not, I'm not!' I said, 'You are, and I'm arguing with you no longer. I'm handing you over to the Master, to Jesus Christ.' He began to scream, and he collapsed all of a sudden. The atmosphere cleared and I began to preach.

* The word of knowledge in operation.

The man rose and said, 'I must go out.'

I said, 'You go where you want, boy—but you want to get right with God first, or the fellow that has left you (you've been delivered) will come back with seven of his friends—he certainly will. You want to get right with God.'

'I must go,' he said. Ten minutes after he came back in and said, 'Friends, I had to go. There's waste ground at the back of this church. I went round there and got down on my knees and I came back to God. I came to Jesus Christ.'

We prayed for him and there and then he got baptised in the Spirit.

I haven't time to tell you the details of other three cases, but in one of them a woman was crawling like a snake up and down the aisle and hissing at everybody.... Then in Edinburgh a man was sitting in the congregation of the Elim Church, shouting, 'Satan's Lord! Satan's Lord!' And two ushers took him out and I went out after him.

He said, 'I don't want anything to do with you; I'm going to take you up to a high mountain and I'm going to throw you down.'

I said, 'Are ye? Well,' I said, 'I don't know how you're goin' tae get me up. And you're certainly no gettin' me up. It's me that's goin' tae throw you down.'

And he ran! He came back into the meeting about a quarter of an hour afterwards and was taken down the stair by two ushers. One of them came up and tipped me on the shoulder saying, 'Are you Danny McVicar?' I said, 'Aye.' He said, 'Well, this man's getting abusive. We'd like you to come down and gie's a hand.' So I went down the stair. As soon as I went down, he jumped up from the chair and said, 'I'm taking you—' I said, 'You're taking me nowhere.' I plunked him down on the chair and put my hand on him, and I said, 'You filthy creature fae hell! Get out!' And that man collapsed.

When he came to, I said to him, 'Who do you think's
Lord?' He said, 'Jesus Christ is Lord.'

My wife said, 'What is this you've got in your pocket?'
His pockets were bulging with paperweights, like marble
eggs, great big ones. 'What are you doin' wi' these?' she
asked. And he said, 'I brought them in to kill the pastor!'

Well, friends, back to my testimony. I made up my
mind there and then I would go to that Pentecostal
church. And the devil said to me, 'Now, simmer down.
Don't do anything rash. You know what your dad says?
It's a mental home for you.' And the devil said to me, 'You
know, seventy-five per cent of Pentecostals—they finish
their lives in a mental home. Don't go there.' But I was
determined to go. I was sure that when the open-air was
finished they would go down to the bottom of Albert
Street, cross Victoria Street, and go right into the Pentecostal church. I had *my* mind made up: I would get
dressed, get a collar and tie on, I would go to the top of the
street, cross Victoria Street and go right down the miners'
rows at the back, and pop in so that nobody would see me.
That was my idea. My oldest brother was out courting.
And in our home there was an old-fashioned chest of
drawers—five drawers. The top drawer belonged to my
brother, and it was filled with all that I needed. Next
drawer was mine—it was empty: nothing in it. He was out
courting; the drawer was locked, but that was easy meat
for me. I'd opened better locks than that. I opened the
lock and got a nice clean shirt out, and collar and tie, and
the back and front studs they had in those days. When I
got the back one in and wrestled with the front, the back
one came out.

As I was wrestling, my dad sat on the chair and looked.
He said, 'Hullo.' I said, 'Aye, what is it?' He said, 'Are ye
emigratin'?' He certainly would have paid my fare!

So I made my mind up, friends, that I would go to
church. When the open-air finished I would just pop out
up to the top of the street. Aye, but God had different

ideas. The open-air finished and they marched down the street. I opened the door and I almost jumped into a woman's arms—the same young woman that preached to me in the street.

She said to me, 'Oh, are you goin' to church?'

I said, 'I am not goin' to church.' That's where I was goin', but I vowed I never would give in to a woman, or change my mind. I've changed my mind, I may tell you that! She walked with me and talked to me, and walked right into the Pentecostal church. God knows what He's doing: two empty seats at the back. She let me go in first, and then she got in, and she put her two knees up against the back of the other seat. And I looked at the two knees. I said, 'I'm in—h'm! I'm certainly in.'

I'll never forget that night. The door opened and out walked the old pastor, Mr. Drysdale. And behind him came a young girl with a hymnbook: she was the singer. Then out came a big fellow who had got saved two years before me: he was one with whom I used to gamble and fight in the pub. There he was: he saw me sitting there, and this was his first gospel message. They had asked him to preach that night. And if ever any young man preached, he did then!

As I sat there, in the middle of the message he stopped, and I was wriggling under conviction. He said, 'I want to ask a personal question. Where will *you* spend eternity?' I was sure he pointed at me. And I said within myself (nobody heard me): 'There's no such a place—a lot o' rubbish.' And he said, 'Aye, ye might be sayin' within yourself, "A lot o' rubbish. There's no such a place."' And I said to this girl next to me, 'Do they read cups in here? Where am I at all? How does *he* know what I'm sayin'?' She said, 'He doesnae know. God knows.'

He went on preaching. And there and then, friends, before he finished, God smote me with terrific conviction. I rose to go out and the girl said to me, 'Where are you goin'?' I said, 'Out to get saved.'

'Glory to God!' she shouts, 'I'll go with ye.'

I said, 'You will not. You'll stay where you are. You're no' makin' a fool o' me here.' And everybody was looking round to see where the argument was.

I didn't wait till the preacher gave an appeal, friends. I left my seat and walked out. I said, 'I want to get saved.' I split Harthill Church in two that night. As I walked down the passage, one half was crying for joy: they'd been praying for me! and the other half was moaning—oh, aye. I just passed a couple of seats, and I heard somebody saying, 'My God, no' him? Surely no'?' Another couple of seats, and I heard them sayin', 'It's Dan McVicar! It's Dan Mc—oh, my God! He'll never get saved!' And when I got down next to the end there were a couple of women sitting, one of them an Irishwoman, and she said, 'He'll blow it (the church) up!' And the other replied, 'The church is comin' to the end o' the road!' Well, it's still there. That was almost sixty years ago, and here I am, saved by the grace of God. But let me tell you, friends, the night that I said I wanted to get saved, the children ran out of the church shouting up the street, 'Dan McVicar's turned a hallelujah!'

The news got home before me, and when I arrived home my dad, a hard, austere man who required careful handling (you had to wrap him in cotton wool) said to me, 'And—where—have—you—been?'

I knew that language. If he had said to me, 'Where was ye?' I'd have been all right. But he said, 'Where have you been?' I knew I was in the kennel, I knew I was in the doghouse, I knew it right away. When I was going out to church I was afraid to tell him. But I said to him now, 'Dad, I've been to a gospel meetin'.' 'So they tell me,' he said, 'and you've got converted.' I said, 'That's right.'

He said to me, 'Well, I want to tell ye something. There's the clock. I'll give you ten minutes to decide your future. You can live wi' me as my son, provided you deny this hellish religion. You've been a misfit fae' ever you

came intae this family'—that's what he said to me.
'You've brought us into shame. You've disgraced the
whole family. But if you deny this hellish religion you can
stay wi' me as my son. If you don't, pack your case and out
you go.'

I said, 'Dad, I never spoke back to you in my life. I've
got to say—'

'Don't preach at me!' he said.

'I'm no' preaching at you,' I said. 'I've no case to pack.
This is what I stand in. But I'm no' denouncin' what I've
got. I go.'

And he made one lurch at me, and he said, 'Yes, and I'll
help you out.' Then an old, ungodly mother stepped
between us and said to my father, 'Just a minute. That's
my boy. I brought that fella into this world, and I'll look
after him. And I want to tell you something: if that boy
goes, I go with him.' And that decided it.

I'd as well have gone, friends. I'm sorry to say this
about the family. We're all right now, but then none of
them would talk to me. Only an old, ungodly mother
would talk to me at the table.

Nine months after I was saved, friends, I married the
girl that preached to me. Well, what would you have
done? What else could I do? I married a good, godly girl.
We spent over fifty years married. We loved each other
and we had a great life. She was saved in the Brethren
before me, and she was my backbone and greatly helped
me in my spiritual life, and I thank God for her. Mr Black
has met her in the church. She was a good girl. (I've
married another good girl, let me tell you that. I've married a prayer warrior. This girl gets up at five o'clock in the
morning. I waken often in the morning at five o'clock and
she's on her knees: she's in touch with the Master.)

Twelve years after I was married, I was a Captain in the
Mines Rescue Team. I have been at most of the disasters
in Scotland, including the big disaster at Knockshinnoch
at Cumnock. I belonged to the Coatbridge Rescue Team.

On one occasion I had been out at a fire in the Lady Colliery for three nights, fighting the fire to save men's lives. When I came home in the morning, my wife said to me, 'You've to go up to your old home.' I said, 'What's wrong?' She said, 'Your mother's dying; she may be dead now. I don't know.' So I said, 'You'd better come with me.'

So I went up and when I opened the door, you could have cut the atmosphere with a knife. No one spoke to me. Here an old, ungodly mother was dying—and they were all saying to her, 'Dae ye ken me, maw? Maw, dae ye ken me?' And she never answered any of them.

And I had a vision of the past, friends. I saw myself in my bedroom at five o'clock in the morning when they were all going to their work and I was still in bed. I had to wait till ten o'clock when the court opened, for I was due to appear there. And an old, ungodly mother used to put her arms round my neck and cuddle me and tears would drop on to my cheeks. As she wept for me, she would say, 'I know you're a bad boy, but I love ye, I love ye, I love ye— and if you get the chance o' a fine today, don't go to prison: you come home to me; I love ye.' And she used to press notes into my hand and say, 'Don't tell anybody that I gave you that money, but you come home to your mother, come home to me.'

And now here she was. I raised my heart to Jesus, and I said, 'O God, give me one chance to talk to her.' The oldest sister had her hands underneath the clothes, and she said, 'Her legs are stone cold—I'm afraid she's gone.'

Then I just prayed to the Lord and I walked forward to the bed and I said, 'Maw, dae ye ken me?' and she sat up in bed, and says, 'That's my boy. That's *Dan!*' I said, 'That's right, maw.'

And you know what she said?

'I want to get saved. Tell me about Jesus. I want to get saved. *Twelve years*—I've waited a long time for ye to come.' I said, 'Maw, I was forbidden ever to come back to this house. But here I am.'

She said, 'Lead me to Christ. Tell me what to do.' And there she said the sinner's prayer. My wife and I led her to Christ. With her arms round my neck, she said, 'Thank God, the burden's gone. The burden's gone, I'm saved, and, Dan, never mind who talks to you or who doesnae talk to you, you go on for God—you've got the best o' it.' And she said, 'I'll see you in the morning!' She died with her arms round my neck—dropped down on the pillow and drew me down. But I thank God she's in the kingdom today.

I was invited back into the family, and attended the funeral. Exactly four years after my mother died, Polkemmet Baths out at Whitburn were being opened—the first pithead baths in Scotland. As oversman I had two tickets for a meal in the canteen after the opening: one for my wife and one for myself. There were other officials too who would be going. Since my wife wouldn't go, I asked my dad and said, 'It'll do you good—you've never seen baths at a minehead: it'll do you good to see them.' You could have taken a lease of my dad's life.

After the baths were opened, an announcement came over the tannoy for those with meal tickets to make their way to the canteen for a meal. 'Come on,' I said to my dad. And walking down the passage in the pithead baths, God spoke to me and said, 'Now's the time to talk to him.' Hard, austere man! I said, 'Dad, I want to say something to you.' 'What is it?' he said. I said, 'You saw my mother gettin' saved. My mother's in heaven now; and dad, if you want to get to heaven, you must confess your sin, you must ask Christ to save ye—if you want to get to heaven and see my mother again.' He was ashen white. He stepped back and he looked at me and he said, 'I know there's a great change in you. But for me, no.' He stamped his foot, and he dropped dead at my feet. I turned him over and tore the collar and tie off him to apply artificial respiration. The minute I put my leg across him, a verse in Proverbs came to me: *He that is ofttimes reproved and hardeneth his neck is suddenly cut off, and that without remedy*. I knew my dad was dead. I knew it. God had given him a chance: it was his last.

You've heard my testimony the night; I've kept the dark, dreadful things out of it. I've proved to you, *If any man be in Christ, he's a new creature*.

I preach all over the place. I'm booked up till part-way into next year. And I've been asked to go to the Philippines for a tent campaign for a month. I'm never sure of my next sleep. For example, six or seven weeks ago I was crawling into bed, tired and just home from a meeting, when the phone rang: a young girl was about to commit suicide. I had to rush to Edinburgh in the car to deal with her—she's in the kingdom tonight. I was in Peebles one night, in Selkirk another, and in Ayr. I'm never sure of a night's sleep—but I tell you this, friends, it's worth it. I live for nothing else than to see souls saved.

And I tell you more, God meets my every need. He called me out at the age of fifty-three, twenty-nine years ago, to leave my job and live for Him by faith. We never had a bank book at that time. We lived by faith, and we never lacked anything. I'll give you an instance of it in a recent matter, to show how God works with us. Our phone bill was £232. And we had nothing, absolutely nothing to pay it. I said to my wife (we'd only been married three months): 'Now don't worry about these things. It's all for God's work, and God'll meet our need.' I'm unorthodox when I pray; when I talk to God I'm unorthodox. I said, 'Right, we'll go into the room and pray about it.' We laid the bill on the bed, I told her to join me in laying her hands on it, and I said, 'Lord, this has arrived at the right address, but the wrong department.' That was all I said. And she said, 'Well—well—' I said, 'Never mind the "well—well," and don't tell anybody about that bill:

don't breathe a word to a soul that that phone bill has arrived. Don't do it.'

Two nights afterwards we went to a meeting miles away from home. There was a fellow sitting in the church, and as I looked at him I was sure I knew him, but I could not remember his name—I'm getting old, you see. At the end of the meeting, I was going to pray for the sick when this fellow came out and said, 'Dan, I've got to go home.' I knew he knew me when he said, 'Dan,' but I didn't like to let him know I didn't know him.

He said, 'I've come wi' a burden.'

I said, 'Well, sit down. I'll pray for you first and let you go if you're in a hurry.' 'No,' he said, 'I've come to gie it to ye.' I said, 'I'm no wantin' a burden.'

'Look,' he said, 'it'll no be a burden to ye; it's a burden to me. For two nights I've wrestled, wrestled with God. God has asked me to give you this, and I've refused and refused. I've wrestled and never had a night's sleep— never had an hour's sleep. There ye are. God bless you,' he said, and out he went. I said, 'Thank you.'

When I came home—you trust a woman!—my wife said to me, 'Did you look in that envelope?' I said, 'No. Listen, girl, we're tired, and the phone might ring. Let's get to sleep.' She said, 'I'll get up and look at it,' but I said, 'You will not. I'll get up.' And when we opened the large envelope, there was £250 in it— £18 to the good. Now my wife can tell you that's true.

We live, friends, for God. We never preach for money, we preach for souls—and God meets our every need. Week after week God meets our every need, and we thank God for it.

NOTE TO READERS

If you would like to enquire further about issues raised in this book or if you feel that the author could be of help, you are invited to write to him at 27 Denholm Street, Greenock, PA16 8RH, Scotland, or telephone 0475 87432.

It may also be of interest to know that the author is normally involved in five conferences in Scotland each year—New Year, Easter, July, August and October. Friends gather from many parts of Britain. An open invitation is extended to all and particularly to those interested in the Baptism in the Holy Spirit and related themes. Details will be provided on enquiry.

By the same author

Reflections on the Baptism in the Holy Spirit

The Baptism in the Holy Spirit...

- Is it something that happens to us all at conversion, or is it a later and separate experience?
- Should people tarry for it?
- Is it the same as sanctification?
- Do tongues always come with it?
- What about men like Spurgeon and Finney? Did they have this experience?

This book honestly faces many of the problems that the Baptism in the Spirit has raised in the minds of so many in our day. The fact that tens of millions of people now claim to have had this experience, which they describe as similar to what happened to the early disciples on the day of Pentecost, makes the book both topical and relevant.

Published in December 1987, the book has proved very popular and is being used to bring people into the experience of which it speaks.

£2.25 UK

By the same author

Reflections on the Gifts of the Spirit

This book speaks of...
- the wonderful operation of the gift of knowledge
- demon exorcism
- miracles of many kinds

Examples are largely drawn from the present day and fall within the personal experience of the author, or of people close to him. Intriguing questions are raised...
- Do demons still speak through human lips?
- Can people receive instantaneous healing?
- Is the future sometimes accurately revealed to God's servants?
- Is angelic ministry real and does it happen today?
- Finally does an ex-Headmaster of a large secondary school, qualified in History (a subject which so often breeds sceptics) believe all these things?

This book was published in March 1988 and contains a number of unusual insights on the gifts in general and on healing, miracles and exorcism in particular.

£2.75

By the same author

Reflections on a Song of Love

(A Commentary on 1 Corinthians 13)

First Corinthians Thirteen has a beauty which has enthralled readers through the ages. It highlights Love and reveals attributes of Christ Himself. It has, however, often been used by opponents of Pentecostal doctrine— quite wrongly, the author maintains. He raises intriguing questions...

- 'Whether there be tongues, they shall cease': did this happen with the close of the canon of Scripture?
- Did knowledge cease at the same time? Will knowledge ever cease in this life, and what will replace it in Heaven?
- When Paul became a man he 'put away childish things'. Did this not include tongues?
- Do Christians generally attain the level of Love taught here, and do they display it in their attitudes to each other, as, for example, when these doctrines deeply divide them?

While the main part of this book gives a wonderful description of Christ and the quality of His Love, these controversial issues are not overlooked. Published in April 1988, this highly original commentary on 1 Corinthians 13 has attracted considerable attention.

£1.25

By the same author

A Trumpet Call
To Women

Is it true that in the Old Testament there were:

Prophetesses?
A Woman Judge?
A Queen (in her own right)?

and in the New Testament:

Prophetesses?   Women Apostles?
Women Teachers?   Women Elders?
Women Evangelists?   Women Deacons?

- What did Paul mean when He taught that in the Church there is neither male nor female?
- And was what the Maréchale said true, 'There is no sex in soul'?
- And are all the spiritual functions which are open to men equally open to women?
- Or should women be in a role subject to men?

This is a highly original piece of writing. The author deals in a biblical way with the question of women ministry. Unlike those who base their case on 'cultural relativism', Mr Black finds his support in the writings of Paul himself. He produces what to many will be an unexpectedly powerful and persuasive case for the ministry of women.

This is a valuable contribution to the current debate.

Published in 1988, this thoughtful and original work has attracted wide attention.

£2.50

By the same author

Consider Him

(Twelve Qualities of Christ)

Like a man gazing into a fathomless pool the author has looked into the infinite deeps of Christ. As the colours of a glorious sky are reflected in ever changing light so the radiance of heaven is reflected in the soul of Christ. We see glory change to glory as we behold His face.

What are the qualities which appear as in a kaleidoscope?

- Peace and Serenity
- Purity and Tranquillity
- Love and Compassion
- Strength and Courage
- Self-effacement and God-centredness
- Power and Glory

The subjects are not treated in a milk and water way. At times the writing cuts like a knife and lays bare our very souls. Our loyalty and commitment are deeply challenged as we are measured, not by our own faulty standards but by His perfection; nor are we expected to stop at intellectual instruction. Change is demanded and expected.

In the second part of the book we see in Miss Jack's life the power of God to effect change. Through crucifixion of the self life and through pain, the Christ nature developed; this always makes for fascinating reading.

Published in 1988, this book should appeal to Christians interested in both sound doctrine and a devotional approach to God.

£2.25

By the same author

Battle for the Body

As in battle rival commanders aim for the same strategic points and seek to exploit each other's weaknesses so in the spiritual war, where the bodies of men are the battlefield, God and Satan aim to secure control of the same vital centres. Each is interested in areas of weakness—Satan that he may enter and destroy—God that He may guard and strengthen. Satan wants the body to be under his control, obeying his commands and ultimately being possessed by him. God wants the same body that it may be wholly His—a channel for His Spirit; holy, strong and pure.

What are the strategic points around which the battle rages?

- Head • Eyes • Ears • Tongue
- Shoulders • Heart • Knees • Backbone
- Hands • Feet • Reproductive Organs

You may be surprised at who really controls these parts of our bodies. Examine the evidence as it is revealed in this searching book.

The second part of the book tells of how battle was waged between God and Satan for one particular life. The story of Rev. John Hamilton has thrilled thousands in Britain, Europe, India and America. It is a remarkable story.

Published in 1988, this book has a practical flavour which will appeal to many.

£2.95

By the same author

The Clash of Tongues: with Glimpses of Revival

This book is divided into two sections. The first deals not only with the regulation of gifts of the Spirit and their relevance for today but also with some of the deeper principles underlying their use. It raises fundamental questions which are sometimes overlooked:

- How can an individual be edified through speaking something which neither he nor his hearers can understand?
- Is there a spiritual means of communication between the human spirit and God which by-passes the intellect but still yields benefit?
- Why did Paul have to make regulations at all? If the gifts are gifts of the Spirit, how can error creep into their use and may the regulations not clash with the direct unctioning of the Spirit upon an individual?
- Tongues, according to verse 2 of 1 Corinthians 14, are Godward. Why then is interpretation so often manward? Surely if God is addressed in one, He will be addressed in the other. Is there Scriptural justification for present-day practice and is there a difference between the tongues of Acts 2, which were understood by foreigners and the 'tongues' of 1 Corinthians 14 which 'no man' understood?

The second part of the book deals with the relationship between revival and Pentecost. It refers to the 1939 and 1949 revivals in Lewis—the first of which has been little publicised although it seems to have been more powerful than the second. A number of people who were much used in this are introduced and the main part of the story is centred on the life and experiences of Mary MacLean, now an old lady of eighty-three, who had quite remarkable visions. Hers is a fascinating story.

An appendix of this book contains evidence that Finney, Moody and Spurgeon were all baptised in the Spirit and all spoke in tongues.

Published in 1988 this book, while of general interest, is expected to appeal particularly to serious students of the New Testament.

£2.75

By the same author

The Incomparable Christ

The first part of this book deals with themes that are amongst the most important that ever engage the minds of men. It concentrates on issues of life and death, of time and eternity. It presents Christ as He really is and faces the reader with the challenge of His life and personality and with the age-enduring and world-wide effect of His teachings. It calls for action. It points out the folly of any man gaining the world at the price of losing his own soul. It faces honestly the questions of Christ's resurrection and that of all men. It speaks of the power of the gospel and deals in a direct way with the doctrine of hell and eternal judgment, and finally it gives practical instruction on the way of salvation.

The second part of the book contains the story of two young ladies, identical twins, who have had their own individual encounters with Christ and have found that He has transformed their lives. Their experiences could encourage others.

Published in 1989, this book, in addition to a particularly interesting presentation of the gospel, provides evidence of the accurate fulfilment of prophecies related to the First Advent. This focuses our thought on the certain fulfilment of the Second Coming.

£2.75

By the same author

Gospel Vignettes

This book focuses attention on various facets of the gospel.
The chapter titles give the flavour:

- Ye Must Be Born Again
- The Life-Giving Water
- The Gospel on the Lips of Paul
- I Am Proud of the Gospel
- Weighed in the Balances of God
- When I See the Blood
- The Brazen Serpent
- The Broad and Narrow Ways
- The Lost Son
- The Lost Sheep
- The Lost Coin
- God So Loved
- Behold I Stand at the Door and Knock
- The Hour of Decision

It also includes the testimonies of three people whose lives
have been transformed by Christ.

Published in June 1989, this book should prove useful to
all who are involved in spreading the gospel.

£2.95

By the same author

Reflections from Abraham

This book outlines spiritual principles seen in the life of Abraham, that great man of God. It deals with...

- His call and ours
- The mountain as distinct from the valley life
- Intercession then and now
- Lot in Sodom
- The sacrifice of Isaac and the way of faith

The second part of the book tells of the action of God in the life of Miss Dorothy Jennings, to whom Abraham has been of particular significance.

£2.50

By the same author

Christ the Deliverer

This book details up-to-date cases of Christ delivering physically and spiritually, from...

- Blindness, Deafness, Manic Depression, ME, Migraine, Post-viral Syndrome, Rheumatoid Arthritis, Skin blotches, Spinal injury, Verrucae
- Phobias and demon torment of various kinds
- Nightmares and hauntings

It speaks of the appearance of angels, touches on revival, and analyses the theory of 'visualisation'.

£2.99

BOOK ORDERS

The books advertised on the previous pages are being made available to Christian booksellers throughout the country, but if you have any difficulty in obtaining your supply, you may order directly from New Dawn Books, c/o 27 Denholm Street, Greenock, Scotland, PA16 8RH.

········ ORDER FORM ········

Please send me the books indicated below:

Quantity	Title	Price
	Reflections on the Baptism in the Holy Spirit	£2.25
	Reflections on the Gifts of the Spirit	£2.75
	Reflections on a Song of Love (A commentary on 1 Cor 13)	£1.25
	A Trumpet Call to Women	£2.50
	Consider Him (Twelve Qualities of Christ)	£2.25
	Battle for the Body	£2.95
	The Clash of Tongues: with Glimpses of Revival	£2.75
	The Incomparable Christ	£2.75
	Gospel Vignettes	£2.95
	Reflections from Abraham	£2.50
	Reflections from Moses: with the testimony of Dan McVicar	£2.99
	Christ the Deliverer	£2.99

Signature ....

Address ....

....

....

When ordering please send purchase price plus 30p per book to help cover the cost of postage and packaging.